THE
POWER
OF
WEAKNESS

THE
POWER
OF
WEAKNESS

EMBRACING *the*
TRUE SOURCE *of* STRENGTH

DAN SCHAEFFER

Discovery House.
from Our Daily Bread Ministries

Discovery House is affiliated with Our Daily Bread Ministries,
Grand Rapids, Michigan.

Requests for permission to quote from this book should be directed
to: Permissions Department, Discovery House, PO Box 3566, Grand
Rapids, MI 49501, or contact us by email at
permissionsdept@dhp.org.

All Scripture quotations, unless otherwise indicated, are from the
New American Standard Bible, updated edition. Copyright © 1960,
1962, 1963, 1968, 1971, 1972, 1973, 1975, 1977, 1995 by The Lockman
Foundation. Used by permission. (www.Lockman.org). Emphasis
(in italics) added by the author.

Interior design by Sherri L. Hoffman

Library of Congress Cataloging-in-Publication Data

Schaeffer, Dan, 1958- author.
  The power of weakness : embracing the true source of strength /
Dan Schaeffer.
       pages   cm
  Summary: "'When I am weak, then I am strong.' Do we really
believe these words penned by the apostle Paul? If so, why do we
often rely on our own wits, strength, and resources when the power
that God holds is so much greater? Does God's power matter if He's
already given us talent and ability? Author Dan Schaeffer explores
these questions and helps us grasp the biblical truth that God longs to
use our limitations to display His greatness. The Power of Weakness
invites you to trust God with your abilities and inabilities and find
relief from the wearying pursuit of success."— Provided by publisher.
  ISBN 978-1-62707-055-3 (paperback)
  1. Christian life. 2. Power (Christian theology) I. Title.
  BV4501.3.S343 2014
  248.4—dc23   2014023511

Printed in the United States of America
Third printing in 2019

To all those wonderful and dear Christians, beset with weaknesses of every kind, who have nevertheless submitted them to God and sought His power. What God has done through your weakness has been an encouragement to me. Your life truly glorifies Jesus.

CONTENTS

CHAPTER ONE

Who Turned Off the Power?

*When God wants to move a mountain, he does not take
a bar of iron, but he takes a little worm. The fact is, we
have too much strength. We are not weak enough. It is not
our strength that we want. One drop of God's strength is
worth more than all the world.* —Dwight Moody

Author and businessman Harvey Mackay told the story of a
ten-year-old boy named Mark who decided to study judo despite
the fact that he had lost his left arm in an automobile accident.

Mark began his lessons with an aged Japanese judo master
and was doing well, but after three months had passed and he
had only been taught one move, he questioned the master. "This
is the only move you'll ever need to know," was the master's
reply.

Perplexed, but trusting, Mark kept training, and several
months later entered his first tournament. Surprising himself,
Mark won the first two matches. The third match was more
difficult, but soon his opponent became impatient and charged.
Mark deftly used his one lone move to win the match.

He was now in the finals, but this time his opponent was
much larger, stronger, and more experienced. Mark was nervous,

and it was showing in the match. The referee, concerned for the boy's welfare, called a time-out. He was about to stop the seemingly imbalanced match when the master intervened and said, "Let him continue."

The match resumed and Mark's opponent made a critical mistake: he dropped his guard. Instantly, Mark used his move to pin his opponent, winning the match and the tournament.

On the way home, Mark reviewed all his matches and moves with his master, finally summoning the courage to ask the question that was foremost on his mind.

"How did I win the tournament with only one move?"

"You won for two reasons," the judo master answered. "First, you've almost mastered one of the most difficult throws in all judo. And second, the only known defense for that move is for your opponent to grab your left arm."[1]

Mark's greatest weakness had become his greatest strength.

Welcome to the point of this book.

Have you ever wondered why so many are drawn to the John Wayne and Clint Eastwood types, or to the Jason Bournes, or to the powerful and fearless superhero characters? Where we would cower in fear or run away, these heroes can and do stand up to the bad guys—without blinking. Though we might decry the violence involved, a part of us wishes we were more like that: bold and brave, confident and powerful. Furthermore, they are usually heroes precisely because they are protecting the "weaklings" who are in danger. Superheroes are popular; super-weaklings are not.

The fact that we have such an appetite for power indicates that it has not been a significant part of our daily experience. Most of us have a generous assortment of weaknesses we'd desperately like to jettison and replace with strengths. Furthermore, we often discover that our weaknesses appear to be growing, not diminishing.

Weakness—Let Me Count the Ways

Most of us feel weak and powerless in more than one area of life. For example . . .

We know our marriage would be better if we could just change, but we can't. It's not that we don't want to or haven't tried. We read the injunctions in Scripture of how a husband and wife ought to act and relate to each other, and we find ourselves coming up short; but we just don't seem to have the power to change.

We are not the parents we always thought we'd be. We thought that being a Christian and having the Bible as a guide would give us a tremendous advantage, but our children seem to bring out the worst in us. Our weaknesses are magnified every day, and even worse, we are now noticing our weaknesses being exhibited in our children. It breaks our heart. We feel so defeated and powerless.

We know that we have an attitude or a habit that is destroying our friendships, but we just can't seem to conquer it. Maybe there was a time when we were resistant to changing, but now we are more honest. We have tried to change. What we're lacking is power.

In our work or occupations, many of us have come to the depressing realization that we're not quite as talented or gifted as we thought we were. Others are passing us by. It is sobering and so very discouraging to watch our dreams and ambitions slowly leak hope like a neglected balloon.

We have tried for years to corral our impure thoughts and pursue holiness, yet we seem to be back where we started. We may look and sound better to others because we've learned how to hide our failures, but we know that inside we are lacking the power to really change. We know that God sees it, and that makes us want to hide from God. We've let Him down. We feel ourselves slipping backward and worry that nothing will stop our descent.

The older we get, the more our bodies fail us. Diabetes, heart problems, bad backs, stomach ailments, incontinence, migraines, worn-out knees and joints, and bad vision weaken us physically. Our bodies are no longer what they used to be. We are becoming more and more limited, and it frightens us. Weakness frightens us.

It is a depressing thought that we are now becoming those who will need care rather than those who give it—that we will become more and more dependent on others for our most basic needs. How can we who are being more and more defined by our weaknesses be prime candidates for experiencing more and more of God's power? How can we be fruitful and productive when we're falling apart?

Along with our physical deterioration, emotionally we are becoming more and more fragile. Smaller things bother us, and our emotional batteries run down quicker than they used to. Stress is a constant companion and fear often paralyzes us. Prayer has not made the fear or fragility of our emotions go away. We might even be resentful toward God for making us this way. If we could begin to experience God's power would it change the way we feel? Would it give us the ability to control our unpredictable emotions?

Even our talents and abilities aren't what they used to be. Age and weakness often diminish these as well.

As I've shared this short list, no matter what your age or life circumstance, I'm sure you have nodded in agreement at least once or twice. Our weaknesses cause us to be afraid, timid, and ashamed. You know it's true.

But the point of this book is not to depress you further about your weakness; it is to help you discover a powerful incentive for embracing your weaknesses. What you will learn will be thoroughly biblical but also counterintuitive, and that will be the primary struggle, because we tend to look at weakness and power in this way:

Weakness = Lack of power

The logic of this seems clear and obvious. But here's the exciting part—it's also dead wrong according to the biblical perspective on weakness. For a Christian the equation is this:

Weakness does NOT = Lack of power

In fact, the whole purpose of this book is to help you not only understand but also begin to embrace this brand-new paradigm:

Personal weakness = Opportunity to experience God's power!

Before you start thinking that this is just another "learn how to be the little train that could" approach and close the book, I want to take you to the words that changed my entire perspective on power and weakness. The man who wrote these words, inspired by the Holy Spirit, also wrote most of the books of the New Testament. He was an apostle who performed miracles through God's power, and who shared doctrinal and theological truths that have guided the church for the last two thousand years. In other words, this fellow is on the short list of the most powerful people in the Bible. He both experienced the power of God and dispensed it—regularly. This is why these words, familiar words that I found myself staring at one day, suddenly didn't make much sense, prompting a second, third, and fourth reading. In fact, I ended up mulling them over for weeks, getting more and more excited the more I realized the implications.

There are times when the truth God is most trying to teach us is the truth we are most resisting. It is our resistance that keeps the truth from making sense. I wrestled with this idea for weeks, and then slowly over the next year began to test this idea out to see if it worked in real life. Frankly, it seemed like a long shot.

Well Content with . . . *What?*

First let me give you a little background. The apostle I'm talking about is Paul, and he was sharing with the Corinthian church that God had given him a "thorn in the flesh," which was some kind of physical ailment (2 Corinthians 12:7). Some commentators believe it was a debilitating eye condition and that it was very unpleasant to look at (see Galatians 6:11; 4:13–14), although this is conjecture. Though Paul had asked God three times to take this "thorn in the flesh" away, God's reply had been clear and unambiguous—Paul was going to have to live with this.

The very apostle God had frequently used to miraculously heal so many of their physical ailments was denied healing of his own! This must have prompted some confusion in Paul—

keep in mind that he prayed this prayer three times, always hoping for a different answer. Yet in God's answer Paul found a wonderful and freeing new way of life, a life-altering approach to accessing the miraculous power of Christ in his life.

> And [the Lord] has said to me, "My grace is sufficient for you, for power is perfected in weakness." Most gladly, therefore, I will rather boast about my weakness, that the power of Christ may dwell in me" (2 Corinthians 12:9 NIV).

This is a popular verse, one most Christians are familiar with, but which I suggest to you is more than it seems. It appears on the surface to simply be encouraging us to admit to our weaknesses because God is glorified through them. Makes sense. And most of us might be thinking about now, "If I glorify God through my weakness, I must constantly be glorifying God, because I have *so many* weaknesses."

But Paul hasn't finished his thought. And it's the next verse that stopped me in my tracks.

> Therefore *I am well content with weaknesses*, with insults, with distresses, with persecutions, with difficulties, for Christ's sake; *for when I am weak, then I am strong* (2 Corinthians 12:10 NIV).

Notice Paul doesn't just say he is "content" with weaknesses, as in "I'll endure them since I can't do anything about them anyway." He says he is "well content." I have always been well acquainted with weaknesses, as I have them in abundance; but I can honestly say that I never considered being well content with them. The same Greek word is used in Matthew 17:5 and Luke 3:22 when, at both Jesus' baptism and transfiguration, God speaks from the heavens and says, "This is My beloved Son, with whom I am well-pleased." Paul uses the same word regarding his weaknesses that the Father did of Jesus when He said He was "well-pleased" with Him.

In my new awareness of this verse, I couldn't escape the question: How could Paul (or anyone) be well content, that is, well . . . pleased with weaknesses? Furthermore, how could Paul proclaim that "when I am weak, then I am strong?" Weakness and strength are opposites. It's like saying, "When I'm hot, then I'm cold." or "When I'm happy, then I'm sad." It's either (1) complete silliness, or (2) a rather crude attempt at hyperbole, or (3) a truth so revolutionary that it will change your life forever. (Just for the record, you'll want to choose door number three.)

Finding Power in All the Wrong Places

Our culture tells us over and over that all the power we will ever need is within us. "Believe in yourself" is the mantra of our generation, and they begin drilling it into us at a tender age. Within ourselves we will find ways, methods, programs, pills, drive, ambition—everything that will make us powerful and successful.

This thinking has also entered the church and weakened it dramatically, for it has disconnected the church from its source of true power. No wonder so many Christians have so little sense of wonder about God and amazement at how intimately involved He is in their lives. We have blocked the main artery that sends His power into our lives!

What would you give to experience the real resurrection

power of Christ in your life, mind, heart, marriage, parenting, job, church, or ministry? Haven't you ever wondered why we who are God's children seem so powerless when God is supposed to be living in our lives and His Spirit dwelling within us? I know I sure have.

What If . . .

What if the path to true power isn't trying harder to be powerful, but giving up the attempt to be powerful altogether? What if God's power could be demonstrated through your life not by trying desperately to overcome your weaknesses but by admitting them and seeking to get out of God's way so He can demonstrate His power through those very weaknesses?

What if your weakness—whatever that might be—is the very vehicle through which God has always wanted to reveal His power? Well, guess what! That's exactly what the Bible teaches us over and over again. This also explains why God didn't remove Paul's weakness.

What if the very way God worked in Paul's life is the same way He works in the lives of all His children? What if "thorns in the flesh" and other kinds of weakness are just disguised opportunities for God to display His power through us? This could certainly change the way we think about a lot of things, couldn't it?

The problem is not that the Bible is keeping this a secret or that we've just found the "secret code" or "magic prayer" to unlocking its hidden truths. The Scriptures are extremely clear on this subject.

The problem lies in us because we've come to believe that weakness is bad and power is good and that we should do everything we can to try to shed all our weaknesses and become powerful. But that is not how God works. Scripture makes it clear that God desires to display His power through our human weaknesses. We see this truth emphasized continuously in the Bible.

> In the wilderness He fed you manna which your fathers did not know, that He might humble you and that He might test you, to do good for you in the end. Otherwise, you may say in your heart, "My power and the strength of my hand made me this wealth." But you shall remember the LORD your God, for it is He who is giving you power to make wealth (Deuteronomy 8:16–18).

> He keeps the feet of His godly ones, but the wicked ones are silenced in darkness; for not by might shall a man prevail (1 Samuel 2:9).

> Both riches and honor come from You, and You rule over all, and in Your hand is power and might; and it lies in Your hand to make great and to strengthen everyone (1 Chronicles 29:12).

> Then Asa called to the LORD his God and said, "LORD, there is no one besides You to help in the battle between the powerful and those who have no strength; so help us, O LORD our God, for we trust in You" (2 Chronicles 14:11).

> You need not fight in this battle; station yourselves, stand and see the salvation of the LORD on your behalf, O Judah and Jerusalem (2 Chronicles 20:17).

For I will not trust in my bow, nor will my sword save me. But You have saved us from our adversaries and You have put to shame those who hate us. In God we have boasted all day long (Psalm 44:6–8).

He gives strength to the weary, and to him who lacks might He increases power. Though youths grow weary and tired, and vigorous young men stumble badly, yet those who wait for the LORD will gain new strength (Isaiah 40:29–31).

Then he said to me, "This is the word of the LORD to Zerubbabel saying, 'Not by might nor by power, but by My Spirit,' says the LORD of hosts" (Zechariah 4:6).

There are many more examples in the Old Testament and we'll visit a number of them. But let's move to the New Testament and see if the pattern holds.

But God has chosen the foolish things of the world to shame the wise, and God has chosen the weak things of the world to shame the things which are strong, and the base things of the world and the despised, God has chosen . . . that no man may boast before God (1 Corinthians 1:27–29).

But we have this treasure in earthen vessels, so that the surpassing greatness of the power will be of God and not from ourselves (2 Corinthians 4:7).

If I have to boast, I will boast of what pertains to my weakness (2 Corinthians 11:30).

Finally, be strong in the Lord and in the strength of His might (Ephesians 6:10).

And what more shall I say? For time will fail me if I tell of Gideon, Barak, Samson, Jepthah, of David and Samuel and the prophets, who by faith conquered kingdoms, performed acts of righteousness, obtained promises, shut the mouths of lions, quenched the power of fire, escaped the edge of the sword, from weakness were made strong (Hebrews 11:32–34).

Whoever serves is to do so as one who is serving by the strength which God supplies, so that in all things God may be glorified through Jesus Christ (1 Peter 4:11).

The verdict seems to be in. God wants us to embrace the very weakness we so detest and to realize that it is through these weaknesses that He desires to demonstrate His power to and through us.

We do need to understand, however, that embracing our weaknesses is not an end in itself. I've encountered many people who, after a few sessions of counseling, consider themselves cured because they are finally able to put a name to their condition, even though nothing has really changed in their lives. They've just become aware of what is wrong with them, and somehow that gives them a sense of peace. In the same way, *recognizing that we have weaknesses is not the same as embracing them for the purpose of seeing God's power displayed through them.*

Never in Scripture does God encourage us to accept our weaknesses for the sake of therapy or self-acceptance. And just to be clear, sin is not weakness—it is disobedience. Our weakness may result in sin, but that does not give us a reason to sin so that God might be glorified in that weakness. That idea was shot down by the apostle Paul when it was first suggested by some Christians in Rome: "What shall we say then? Are we to continue in sin so that grace may increase? May it never be! How shall we who died to sin still live in it?" (Romans 6:1–2).

The problem with this idea of embracing weakness is that it is not just counterintuitive, it is also counter-cultural. And like it or not, we all live in a culture. To go in the opposite direction of conventional wisdom is unnatural and uncomfortable, and we are loathe to do it. But sometimes that is the direct path to deliverance.

Years ago there was a movie called *The Poseidon Adventure*. In this movie, the ocean liner SS *Poseidon* encounters a terrible storm at sea and flips over, but because of the air trapped in the ship, it floats upside down. Most of the passengers who survive the initial onslaught get disoriented and try to escape by climbing the steps to the top deck. Unfortunately, the top deck is now deep under water, and in trying to get to the top, they actually go down into the water and drown. Only those who do what is counterintuitive survive. A small group of people descend into the dark belly of the ship until they reach the hull. By "going down," they reach the ocean's surface. Rescuers finally hear them and they are saved.

Our world, which has chosen to disobey God and live life apart from Him, has been thrown upside down. To survive, we must go in the opposite direction.

Our world tells us: "Embrace your strengths and overcome your weakness." Only in the Scriptures are we encouraged to embrace our weaknesses and through them experience a power we could never know otherwise. This is not our own power, but the power of the risen Christ. And once you have experienced the power of God in your life, I promise that you will never be satisfied with anything less.

This book is for those who consider themselves powerless failures, as well as for those who are successful in many people's eyes but realize they have never (or rarely) experienced the real power of God in their lives. It is for those who have come to believe that the power of God is more hyperbole than reality in their lives. This book is for those who truly long to see tangible experiences of God's power in their life—on a regular basis.

But I must issue this warning! The path to experiencing the power of God requires humility and a willingness to correctly assess and confess your personal weaknesses before the God of all power. This pathway leads to power for living, for seeing amazing change take place in your life and the lives of those you love through the very weakness you have grown to despise. It leads to power for radical and unexpected ministry victories. But it will take some learning and, frankly, some unlearning. There is a tremendous upside to weakness. Let's find out what it's all about.

CHAPTER TWO

We're Not Alone

You needn't worry about not feeling brave. Our Lord didn't—see the scene in Gethsemane. How thankful I am that when God became man He did not choose to become a man of iron nerves; that would not have helped weaklings like you and me nearly so much. —C. S. Lewis[1]

Throughout Scripture God affirms the few, the small, and the insignificant who live by faithfulness rather than forcefulness . . . God is willing to spare Sodom and Gomorrah if only ten righteous people can be found. Christ is present where two or three gather in His name. The widow's mite is the largest gift. The boy with a few loaves and fish provides food for thousands. Jesus fed five thousand but only shared the Lord's Supper with the Twelve and was revealed to the two in Emmaus as they broke bread. The mustard seed, the pearl of great price, the leaven in the loaf, the lost sheep and coin, the sparrows, and the numbered hairs on a person's head are all powerful signs that small can be theologically mighty.

—David Ray[2]

Before we go any further, let's stop and read another passage that gets too little attention these days. It is a description given by the apostle Paul *of* the Corinthians *to* the Corinthians. In these days of flattery and promotion, these words may sound a little strange.

> For consider your calling, brethren, that there were not many wise according to the flesh, not many mighty, not many noble; [Ouch!] but God has chosen the foolish things of the world to shame the wise, and God has chosen the weak things of the world to shame the things which are strong, and the base things of the world and the despised God has chosen, the things that are not, so that He may nullify the things that are, so that no man may boast before God (1 Corinthians 1:26–29).

Foolish, weak, base, and despised. Yes, believe it or not, Paul was referring to the Corinthians! He makes it unapologetically clear to the Corinthian church that there weren't a lot of impressive people (humanly speaking) who were called by God; in fact, it appears God wanted it made clear that He chose the weak. Think about the implications of that for a moment. Christianity grew in spite of the fact that, at least at first, its main adherents were weak and unimpressive and even despised. Furthermore, this choosing of the weak was done by divine design, "so that no [one] may boast before God."

What made the early church different? The power of God displayed clearly in the lives of people. The power of God was a consuming and ever-present reality to the early church.

Frankly, the more you read the Bible the more you will

recognize that Paul is not just describing the Corinthians here; he is describing those who have trusted in God throughout the centuries.

You can argue with ideas, you can challenge beliefs, you can roll your eyes in weariness at new programs and fads in church, but when someone's life is drastically and permanently changed, people have no recourse but to pay attention. Something powerful has happened.

Launching Power from an Unfamiliar Place

We frequently view the "heroes" of the Bible through rose-colored glasses. The Bible never does that. In Hebrews 11, which is the Hall of Faith for Old Testament saints, we read about some of those folks who did amazing things. After the writer of Hebrews has recited many of the things God's people had done in Old Testament times (Hebrews 11:1–31), he almost sighs from exhaustion as he writes:

> And what more shall I say? For time will fail me if I tell of Gideon, Barak, Samson, Jephthah, of David and Samuel and the prophets, who by faith conquered kingdoms, performed acts of righteousness, obtained promises, shut the mouth of lions, quenched the power of fire, escaped the edge of the sword . . . (vv. 32–34).

I'm going to stop here for a moment as we consider this daunting list. Gideon faced thousands of enemies of Israel with three hundred handpicked men. Barak defeated the Canaanites with the help of the prophetess Deborah. Samson defeated Israel's enemies in his last noble moment of life. Jephthah was used of God to defeat the Ammonites and to punish the tribe

THE POWER OF WEAKNESS

of Ephraim. David was the greatest of all Israel's kings, the only
soldier brave enough to face Goliath and a courageous warrior
until the end. Samuel was a great prophet and used mightily of
God in the lives of both Saul and David. Then the author just
lumps all the prophets and their incredible acts into one word,
"prophets." Think of Elijah and the 450 prophets of Baal, of
Elisha, of Jeremiah and Isaiah and all their righteous acts and
courage.

But after the writer lists all of the amazing accomplishments of these men and women, he says this: "from weakness
[they] were made strong" (11:34).

These great men and women of faith were not strong to
begin with. Strong is what God made them "from weakness."
Gideon and his army of three hundred had very little to do
with the victory as God defeated His enemies. David, who
made a name for himself as a great warrior by defeating the
mighty giant Goliath, was a smallish shepherd boy with a sling.
In fact, if we continue reading, we begin to see what God was
able to do through their weakness: "[they] became mighty in
war, put foreign armies to flight. Women received back their
dead by resurrection; and others were tortured, not accepting
their release, so that they might obtain a better resurrection"
(Hebrews 11:34–35).

Notice the word *became*. To become something means that
you weren't that something before. These folks became mighty;
they became strong enough in faith to receive their dead back by
resurrection, to endure torture and many other things. Something happened to them that human strength or ability could
not account for.

The power of Christ launches from our weakness, not our
strength!

Anti-heroes of the Faith

God has always worked powerfully and exclusively through human weaknesses. Because He is omnipotent, all power ultimately finds its source in Him—and He dispenses it as He will.

As we think about this, we will find it educational to go back and visit Moses and the miracles before Pharaoh in the book of Exodus. But first, let's read Moses's sterling resume, which he shared gladly with God: "Then Moses said to the Lord, 'Please, Lord, I have never been eloquent, neither recently nor in time past, nor since You have spoken to Your servant; for I am slow of speech and slow of tongue" (Exodus 4:10).

This was Moses's confession after God recruited him to represent Him before Pharaoh. He was slow of speech and tongue—read, he just wasn't a good speaker. At all! He was literally begging God not to use him.

How many modern politicians, activists, or leaders of nations or companies are really bad speakers? It seems to be almost universally true that to lead people effectively you need to be an effective communicator. Even back in his day Moses was not ignorant of this truth and was trying to convince God of its importance. In what Moses considered the most important qualification for the job—he stunk!

God answered Moses simply and clearly: "Who has made man's mouth? Or who makes him mute or deaf, or seeing or blind? Is it not I, the LORD? Now then go, and I, even I, will be with your mouth, and teach you what you are to say" (Exodus 4:11–12).

Basically God said, "Moses, I know all about you. I made you, remember? Go do what I have asked you to do and I'll be there to help you."

Pharaoh was a man of power, impressed by power. Nothing short of an encounter with a greater power would convince him.

Not Moses's golden oratory, but God's power working through Moses. As Moses and his brother Aaron prepared to go before Pharaoh for the first time, God told them, "When Pharaoh speaks to you, saying, 'Work a miracle,' then you shall say to Aaron, 'Take your staff and throw it down before Pharaoh, that it may become a serpent'" (Exodus 7:9).

God didn't tell Moses to have Aaron practice throwing the staff down, or to do research on the kinds of staffs most likely to turn into serpents. Ironically, the Egyptian wise men and sorcerers did practice that art and after many years of experience were able to duplicate the feat through smoke and mirrors. But Aaron's serpent swallowed up all the pretenders. That little display was designed to get the attention of the smoke-and-mirrors crowd.

When God told Moses He would strike the Egyptians with frogs, Moses didn't send a team to find out where frogs would be at that time of year, what kind of frogs multiplied the quickest, or which would cause the most devastation per square acre. When Moses was told that God would turn the Nile to blood, he had no idea how God was going to do that, and no earthly way of helping Him.

God wasn't asking Moses to create these miracles—His "signs and wonders" (Exodus 7:3). He planned to do that. All of that. He didn't need any help from Moses or Aaron. But He did ask them to show up, share His message, and then act in faith (remember, Moses predicted miracles that had yet to occur—a daunting task to be sure). God was going to do a number of miracles that were precisely that—supernatural—unexplainable.

A Bad Idea That Sounds Good

The Scriptures remind us that God is the same yesterday, today, and forever (Hebrews 13:8). He does not change

(Malachi 3:6). And throughout the Scriptures we see God doing miracles without human assistance. It's not that He doesn't ask people to do anything. He does. But over and over again what He asks of us is to show up and believe—in spite of the odds, or how we feel about ourselves, or what our obvious weaknesses are. His goal is that we might see Him and His power at work.

But these days a new idea reigns supreme: We can do this! We have done research, consulted all the experts, have undergone extensive training, and have clearly observable talents and proven abilities. On top of that, we've got drive and ambition. We disdain weakness and praise organization, resources, and methodology. From raising children with the latest methods to starting and growing churches according to the latest strategies and approaches, we believe deep down in our hearts that we can do this!

We plan and strategize to match our talents and abilities to the task so that our strengths are paraded and our weaknesses minimized. In fact, we are so careful about this that many are discouraged from entering certain professions, jobs, or roles based on psychological or personality tests that "red flag" areas where they are too high a risk for failure.

By these standards, I can't help but wonder if Moses, such a terrible and reluctant speaker with such an obvious self-esteem issue, would have ever been selected to lead a nation of a million or so people.

Abraham was promised that he would be the father of a nation when he was ninety-nine years old and his wife, Sarah, was ninety. That's either a case of really bad divine timing or an example of weakness.

Joseph was sold into slavery by his brothers, became a slave to Potiphar, and later became a prisoner in Pharaoh's prison. Joseph was in a very weak position. But God didn't tell him to plan a coup against Pharaoh within the prison walls. He simply allowed Joseph to be used to reveal the meaning of a dream to another prisoner. After that, Joseph continued to languish in prison. Weakness. Discouragement. Helplessness. Hopelessness. Until one day Pharaoh had a dream and found that one of his formerly imprisoned aides, now back in his good graces, remembered a fellow named Joseph who interpreted dreams.

David was a young shepherd with no military training, so small he couldn't even fit into Saul's armor. Yet God used him to defeat the greatest military warrior of the age, Goliath. One sling and five smooth stones. Go back and read the description of Goliath in 1 Samuel 17 and then remember: one sling and a few rocks. And the stone had to directly hit the only vulnerable area on Goliath's helmeted head, and with just the right amount of velocity to do the job. Weakness, not strength.

Daniel was a slave in a foreign land forced to work for his conquerors. He and his three companions—Shadrach, Meshach, and Abed-nego—were totally at the mercy of the government and a highly volatile and egotistical king. Thrown into a den of hungry lions (weakness), thrown into a fiery furnace for failing to bow down to Nebuchadnezzar's idol (weakness)—these were not positions of strength.

God's power is launched from weakness, not from strength. On purpose.

No Other Explanation

We could give more examples, but the point has been made. God has shown over and over that His power is launched from our weakness. Why? Because the power of God is seen most clearly when there is no other explanation that will do justice to the events.

If I'm a persuasive and winsome speaker and many are moved by my messages, who is likely to get the credit? But if I'm a lousy speaker and yet through my unimaginative and even at times complicated messages the Roman world is turned upside down, who is likely to get the credit? That was Paul's point. It is what God was trying to tell Paul each of the three times he begged God to remove his thorn in the flesh. God's specific response was, "My grace is sufficient for you, for power is perfected in weakness." Paul's response was ultimately, "Most gladly, therefore, I will rather boast about my weaknesses, so that the power of Christ may dwell in me" (2 Corinthians 12:9).

Paul was willing to accept that his thorn in the flesh would not be removed because his "reward" for that was to experience the power of Christ dwelling in him. Now let's just stop here. How many of us can say we have clearly and honestly experienced the power of Christ dwelling in us? I think many of us would be hard-pressed to know what that even means. Does simply bragging about how weak I am in different areas mean that Christ's power is dwelling in me? The answer is no.

Paul wanted to see and feel God work in his life in such a way that it would be unmistakable. He wanted to know that God was working through his weaknesses to accomplish great things for the kingdom of God, so that God alone would get the credit and glory.

Paul goes on to list the areas of his weaknesses, insults, distresses, persecutions, and difficulties. When he does that, he proclaims again in a new way, "For when I am weak, then I am strong." When his skills and abilities aren't up to the task at hand, he is strong for he realizes that Christ wants to demonstrate

His power through him. When he is constantly insulted for his presence, his message, even his person, he is strong, for then Christ wants to demonstrate His power through him. When he is being persecuted and is unable to escape, then he is strong, for Christ will intercede for him.

When life got really difficult for Paul, which was most of the time, he learned to relax because though he could not handle it all, he didn't have to. Christ wanted, through that difficulty, to demonstrate His power in a remarkable way through this weak vessel known as Paul.

Power Perfected in Weakness

If I feel that all my training, all my preparations, have adequately prepared me to finish a task successfully, I do not rely upon the power of Christ to help me. In short, when I don't feel weak, when I don't know that I really am weak, I don't seek the power of Christ in my life. This is the downside to our view of our own human strength: it blocks the flow of the power of Christ to us.

I can make my marriage work because I'm an intelligent and rational person, I know all the Bible verses about marriage, and besides, there are multitudes of marital helps I can consult.

I can raise great kids who love God because I'm a strong Christian, I love my children, and I've read all the experts.

I can do ministry effectively because I love God, I have obvious spiritual gifts, I've been trained, and I've read all the experts and the latest cutting-edge approaches.

I can be successful in life because I have tremendous drive and ambition.

I can beat my moral weaknesses because I have a strong will and am self-disciplined.

I can reach all my goals in life because I have physical and mental advantages others don't have.

I can _____. (You fill in the blank.)

At first, Paul just wanted his weakness removed. That's a first and natural reaction for all of us. We don't like weakness, because it is embarrassing to us. We are proud of our "can dos," and we are usually ashamed of our weaknesses and try to hide, not publicize them. Yet Paul said that although he had seen amazing visions of heaven, he would only boast about one thing, and that one thing would be "in regard to my weaknesses" (2 Corinthians 12:5).

Why would any intelligent person boast about his weaknesses? Well, what if, all of a sudden, you began to experience the power of Christ in such a powerful way that it made you weep for joy? And what if you began to realize that your weaknesses were the very channels through which God has always wanted to make His power known in your life? What if time after time you witnessed God do something powerful through your greatest weakness? What if you realized that all your striving, all your efforts at "success," all your drive and ambition, all your education and training had gotten you nowhere—but one day God showed His power through you in a way that had never happened before?

That is what Paul meant when he said that God's power is perfected in weakness.

We can grow so very, very weary chasing success.

We long to be experiencing the reality of God's power through our lives, but so often we have been chasing it the wrong way. Our culture has greatly influenced us, to be sure, but the truth is that we have taken our eyes off the Scriptures, which clearly tell us that God desires to work in us to show His power—and to work in such a way that He alone will get the credit for the amazing things that are accomplished. He wants to be the primary attraction in our lives.

We still have quite a lot to learn. But if we don't understand that God desires to work through our greatest weaknesses, the weaknesses we have right now, we can't move forward.

An Honest Problem

What are your greatest weaknesses? Just now, as you entertained that thought, you experienced one of our greatest problems: honesty. The moment you began to think about your weaknesses, something inside you recoiled. It is a protective mechanism designed to protect our self-image, our pride, our vanity. It is painful to admit that our abilities aren't as impressive as we want them to be or that we don't always know what we need to do next.

Most of our weaknesses are carefully guarded secrets within us—secrets that the whole world already knows. I might think I'm the best husband in the world, but just to play it safe I won't mention this little fact to my wife. I might think I qualify to be Father of the Year, but I'm not likely to poll my kids about this (unless they're still toddlers—ah, those were the days!) I might feel that my greatest strength is my leadership ability or my preaching, but those who listen to me and watch me minister know otherwise.

I'm average. Barely. Some days I'm not even that. Sound familiar? The faintest suspicion that this might be true terrifies us because we believe it pre-determines us. Without great giftedness, how can we ever do great things, or even the things that are expected of us? Expectations are the black light that illuminates so many of our weaknesses.

Just think of all the areas in which we expect ourselves to be strong. We need to be:

A good spouse	A good caregiver
A good parent	A good friend
A good son	A good servant of Christ
A good daughter	A good witness of Jesus
A good employer	A good financial steward
A good employee	A physically healthy person

Any of the above make you nervous? And this isn't anything like a complete list.

There are two ways to rate ourselves in the above categories: (1) the safe way, and (2) the honest way. Most of us choose the safe way because we are afraid of appearing weak. But weakness is not failure—it is simply weakness, and it is standard equipment on all human models. This doesn't mean, however, that we're weak all the time in everything. That would be truly depressing.

Keep in mind that both weakness and power existed simultaneously in Paul's life. The same thing was true of our Lord; both weakness (His humanity) and power (His divinity) existed simultaneously in His life. Isn't the cross the ultimate example of power being perfected through weakness? "Being found in appearance as a man, He humbled Himself by becoming obedient to the point of death, even death on a cross" (Philippians 2:8).

Earl Palmer tells the story of sailors in distress in the South Atlantic.

The Amazon River is the largest river in the world. The mouth is 90 miles across. There is enough water to exceed the combined flow of the Yangtze, Mississippi, and Nile Rivers. So much water comes from the Amazon that they can detect its currents 200 miles out in the Atlantic Ocean. One irony of ancient navigation is that sailors in ancient times died for lack of water . . . caught in windless waters of the South Atlantic. They were adrift, helpless, dying of thirst. Sometimes other ships from South America who knew the area would come alongside and call out, "What is your problem?" And they would exclaim, "Can you spare us some water? Our sailors are dying of thirst!" And from the other ship would come the cry, "Just lower your buckets. You are in the mouth of the mighty Amazon River." [3]

Tragically, too often we are just like those sailors. There is no shortage of God's power; it surrounds us on all sides. The Scriptures give us example after example of God demonstrating His power through weak people who were encouraged, or prodded, to just put their buckets over the side and reel it in. It is clear from the biblical accounts that God wants to demonstrate His power through our weakness. The only thing gumming up the works is that we don't know how to access His power, or we think it is some spiritual secret that we can only learn after we reach Moses's status.

We've become accustomed to denying our weakness and trying to overcome it. There are reasons for this. Why is it so hard to admit our weakness? Let's examine this idea in the next chapter.

CHAPTER THREE

Why It's So Hard to Admit Our Weaknesses

Knowing your own strength is a fine thing. Recognizing your own weakness is even better. What is really bad, what hurts and finally defeats us, is mistaking a weakness for a strength. —SYDNEY J. HARRIS

Author, speaker, and former atheist Lee Strobel relates an experience that transformed him when he was a young Christian.

The sun was scorching. I found a patch of shade under an expansive tree and sat cross-legged on the brown and brittle grass. I was visiting the predominantly Hindu province of Andhra Pradesh in Southeast India as a volunteer writer for an Indian ministry. My task was to produce articles about the thousands of people who were crowding into exciting nighttime rallies to hear the message of Jesus. But today was something new: an American pastor was going to stop by and speak at a modest event in a sparsely populated farming community at noon, when it was hot and people were generally busy in the fields. Frankly, I was skeptical that anybody would show up.

Half a dozen Indian musicians began playing music to attract a crowd. I picked up a tambourine and tried to keep the beat of the syncopated tunes. (Thankfully, nobody captured this on video, and YouTube didn't exist yet!) Soon some onlookers began to gather. Fifteen minutes later there were twenty-five people who were sitting on the grass, apparently curious why anyone would come to this remote and seemingly forgotten locale. The musicians played song after song, nervously looking around for the pastor. He was late and there was no sign of him.

The people were getting antsy; the music could only keep them from going back to their fields a little while longer. Finally one of the musicians bent down and whispered to me: "One more song, then you give the sermon." I glared at him. *"Me?"* I nearly shouted in a panic. I was a journalist, not a preacher. I had never given a sermon, especially half way around the world. In fact, I had never spoken about my faith to any group of people. The last time I had given a speech was in high school. I had no notes, no message, no training, and no experience. What I *did* have—in abundance—was paralyzing stage fright. What could I say? How could I speak to these Hindus who were so culturally different from me?

The music stopped. There was absolute silence. Twenty-five pairs of quizzical eyes bored in on me. My palms began to sweat, my knees shake, my heart palpitate. Fighting back waves of nausea, I slowly rose to my feet, my mind churning wildly to come up with something to say as the interpreter took his position, ready to translate my words into Telugu. "So . . ." I began, offering a weak smile. "Hindus, are you?"

The interpreter shot me a perplexed glance as if to say, *Is that really how you want to start?* I was tempted to tell him, "Just deal with it. I didn't *ask* to be up here!" But when I didn't say anything, he dutifully translated my words. There was no discernible reaction from the small gathering. I really can't recall the details of what I said next. I think I talked about Jesus. I'm pretty sure I told them why I loved him and how he had forgiven all of my wrongdoing—past, present, and future. Chances are I told the story of how I came to faith.

When it came time to share the gospel, my mind was a jumble. I tried to remember some Bible verses and give some coherent explanation for Jesus' death on the cross. I attempted to explain why these lower caste Hindu laborers should abandon the only religion they had ever known and risk the rejection of their family, friends, and community by embracing Christ. Instead I simply rambled in disjointed sentences.

I felt like an utter failure. I had an overwhelming and oppressive sense that I had made a complete mess of things. At the end I said something like this: "I know it would be a great sacrifice for you to receive Jesus. I know this can be dangerous around here, so don't even consider it if you're not ready. Believe me, I'll understand. But we're going to play one more song while I pray. Then after you've had a chance to think about it, if you want to put your trust in Christ, I'll help you do that."

I folded my hands, shut my eyes, bowed my head, and in dejection and despair offered a silent prayer—of *repentance.*

Oh, Father, I'm so sorry! I know I'm not Billy Graham. I know I'm not qualified to give a sermon. I don't deserve to be doing something this important. I'm sure I botched it. Please forgive me for thinking that a sinner, a nobody, a former atheist like me, could represent you to these precious people. They deserve so much better. If you just let me get out of here safely, I promise you I'll never do this again! Please, please forgive me.

With that, I opened my eyes, looked up—and gasped! Twelve men and women had stood to their feet and stepped forward to receive Christ, tears flowing down their cheeks. It was like an electric shock jolted my body. And I knew at that moment that I would never be the same.

If that musician had given me a choice, I never would have opened my mouth that day. Had there been a graceful way to escape it, I certainly would have. No question I was unqualified and unprepared. Yet on that sizzling afternoon in the middle of the grassy countryside on the far side of the planet, God evicted me from my cocoon and sent me soaring on a completely undeserved adventure. I never could have anticipated that within five years of that incident I would be a teaching pastor at one of the largest churches in America, speaking there and around the country to thousands of spiritually curious people. *But God knew.*[1]

Let's go back to a counter-intuitive, counter-cultural statement made by the apostle Paul: "If I have to boast, I will boast of what pertains to my weakness" (2 Corinthians 11:30). Was Paul engaging in hyperbole? Was he just writing these words for effect?

The incredible suffering Paul had endured, which he had just detailed in verses 23 through 28 of this chapter, are a litany of his personal moments of terrible vulnerability and weakness. Yet at the end, the crescendo of this moving section, he repeats the chorus he was so fond of: "If I must boast, I will boast of my weakness." There is no sense of false humility here. Another far more important principle was being put into play in his life, a principle that is life-changing.

Paul's goal was not to draw attention to his lowliness, but rather to shine the spotlight on the place where God's power was most going to evidence itself in his life. God had taught Paul that His power would be evident in his weakness, and Paul wanted to experience the power of God. Author J. I. Packer hints at this truth in our own lives.

We grow up into Christ by growing down into lowliness . . . Off-loading our fantasies of omnicompetence, we start trying to be trustful, obedient, dependent, patient, and willing in our relationship to God. We give up our dreams of being greatly admired for doing wonderfully well. We begin teaching ourselves unemotionally and matter-of-factly to recognize that we are not likely ever to appear, or actually to be, much of a success by the world's standards. We bow to events that rub our noses in the reality of our own weakness, and we look to God for strength quietly to cope . . . It is impossible at the same time to give the impression both that I am a great Christian and that Jesus Christ is a great Master. So the Christian will practice curling up small, as it were, so that in and through him or her the Savior may show himself great. That is what I mean by growing downward.[2]

How many of us struggle to hide our lack of omni-competence? We often spend a great deal of time defending our competence, even in areas where we are truly suspect. It is a self-defense mechanism, almost instinctual in our sinful human natures which do not easily take criticism.

Ironically, in the passage prior to 2 Corinthians 11:30, Paul had been defending himself to the Corinthians against the "false apostles" who were attacking him in Corinth. Yet even in his defense, he took a counter-intuitive approach. He gladly, willingly, pointed out his weaknesses to the Corinthians. If his weaknesses drew attention to God's power, he would not only admit to them—he would proudly call attention to them.

Imagine the Corinthians comparing the false apostles—who were constantly touting their strengths—with Paul who, instead of trying to gloss over his weaknesses, or boasting how he had overcome them, pointed to them as prime examples of the place where God's power would be demonstrated through his life.

Most of us don't mind admitting a weakness in those areas of our life that pose no threat to our pride or sense of self-sufficiency.

"I'm no longer the athlete I once was."

"I'm a little heavier than I used to be."

"My memory's not what it used to be."

These are safe, almost easy (almost) admissions, usually made with a bit of a smile. Even the best athletes reach a peak and start to decline. And who isn't a little heavier than they were ten or twenty years ago? I can't even remember what the third admission was.

Besides, as long as we feel sufficiently strong or competent in other areas, we don't feel as threatened admitting weaknesses in "safe" areas. But this is simply a willingness to admit weaknesses. Paul speaks of boasting about them, of pointing them out to others on purpose and with a purpose, and even with a strange pride.

But why, generally speaking, is it so hard for us to admit or minimize our weaknesses? There are a number of reasons, and although this list will certainly not be exhaustive, I think it is representative of most of us. We begin with fear and trembling since these are issues near and dear to all of our hearts.

Because It Will Threaten Our Self-image

Most, if not all of us use our self-image as a protection for our ego. The common mantra of our society is "I don't care what anyone else thinks." You've heard celebrities, sports stars, and others say this over and over. They might as well follow that up with, "and I've got two heads." It would be about as believable. Everyone cares what other people say about them. They may teach themselves to continue on their course in the face of criticism, but don't kid yourself—everyone cares what others say about them.

As a result, we tend to be very careful about what information we let out to others about ourselves. I have been a pastor for many years. Over those years I have met literally thousands of new people who have visited the churches I've pastored. And I have yet to have anyone come up to me and say, "Hello, Pastor Dan, I'm Frank. I'm new at your church and I just want you to know a little about me. I was divorced eight years ago because, frankly, I was horrible to live with. I abused my wife verbally and ignored her needs and our children, and she finally had enough and left me. It's probably because I'm very self-centered and not all that competent in my vocation, so I felt inadequate at work and in society. I've had a number of immoral relationships with women since then because I'm not good at interpersonal relationships. I also haven't kept up much with my children, and I've struggled with pornography for about fifteen years. I can be a real jerk at times and tend to be highly critical of others. I'm not very faithful at church either. I tend to show up when I'm feeling most guilty about my life. Just FYI."

I do frequently find these things out, but usually only over time as weaknesses are shared sliver by sliver, or when a crisis occurs in their lives where the value of secrecy no longer outweighs the need they have for help. Only once in my entire life has a person come to me with a significant weakness right up front, confessing it and asking me to help hold him accountable. I admire that person more than I can say, and he has proven to be an example to me of true strength.

Paul reminds us in his letter to the Romans that wisdom begins with thinking rightly about ourselves. "For through the grace given to me I say to everyone among you not to think more highly of himself than he ought to think; but to think so as to have sound judgment, as God has allotted to each a measure of faith" (Romans 12:3).

We hide our weaknesses from others because they will affect the way others view us, and we want to make good impressions, perhaps better than we deserve.

Because We Are Afraid It Will Hold Us Back

Life teaches us many things, and some of them are hard lessons learned. At least once in the past most of us have probably admitted a weakness, or had a weakness become known about us, that has kept us out of a position or opportunity we desired. If we didn't lose the opportunity, we were definitely viewed differently from that point on.

Years ago, when I was fresh out of seminary, I was seeking to start a church. I was encouraged to partner with a local para-church organization that helped start new churches for denominations and was introduced to several men who would work with me. As we got to know each other, they asked me questions, and my answers caused them to become very excited about the project. They felt I was "just the kind of guy they were looking for." We began to work together and plan for this project. Part of the process involved me taking a number of tests that would help to pinpoint areas of strength and weakness. I took the tests and gave the results to my mentor.

The next day I received a phone call from him. Had I been upset emotionally when I took the test? Had I been depressed about something recently? No, I told him, everything was fine. He asked me to come in and discuss the results of the test with me. When I arrived, my mentor looked like his favorite dog was on life support. The excitement he had previously evidenced about the project and working together was gone as he explained my test results. After listening to his explanation of what the test said about my personality I replied, "That sounds about right." The look on his face told me he had just disconnected the life support on his dog.

Apparently I had tested out all wrong for a church planter. A successful church planter, I was told, scored highly in different categories than I did. After that I was ushered into the president of the organization's office who asked if I really thought I was cut out to be a church planter. Now I was feeling like *my* dog had just died. I was exactly the same person I had always been, the one they had been all excited about a week ago, but now I was being assured that I didn't have what it took.

I believed wholeheartedly that God was leading me to plant a church. And I decided after much heart-wrenching soul-searching to start the church without them. But I also learned a lesson: people often can't look beyond your weaknesses; they make decisions about what you can do based on your weaknesses.

This is one of the reasons we are so fearful of being honest with others about our weaknesses. We're afraid those honest confessions will create a glass ceiling for us in their minds. We can be locked out of opportunities if people think our weakness is a liability. We are pigeon-holed before we even begin. As a result, we determine to put our best foot forward.

We're not only afraid of admitting our weaknesses to others, but to ourselves as well. If I admit a weakness, can I still pursue what excites me? Will I eventually talk myself out of even trying because of my weakness? We can often feel that it's safer emotionally to go into denial.

Back to the apostle Paul—let's listen to his introduction to the Corinthian church. It is illuminating.

> And when I came to you, brethren, I did not come with superiority of speech or of wisdom, proclaiming to you the testimony of God. For I determined to know nothing among you except Jesus Christ, and Him crucified. I was with you in weakness and in fear and in much trembling, and my message and my preaching were not in persuasive words of wisdom, but in demonstration of the Spirit and of power, so that your faith would not

rest on the wisdom of men, but on the power of God"
(1 Corinthians 2:1–5).

Somehow the words "apostle" and "weakness, fear, and trembling" don't seem to belong together. I can't help but wonder what the Corinthian church thought when Paul showed up—the mighty apostle of Jesus Christ. He was physically weak, admittedly fearful, and even trembling. Today, this guy would never have an international TV ministry . . . yet God used him to turn the world upside down.

Some things in life are so precious to us that we dare not even entertain thoughts or confessions of weakness that could derail our plans. We will somehow overcome them, we tell ourselves. We'll get better. We'll be the exception. We're special.

We're afraid that others might use knowledge of our weaknesses against us—and in fact, that's a real possibility. It certainly was for Paul. Responding to criticism from the false apostles, Paul wrote, "For they say, 'His letters are weighty and strong, but his personal presence is unimpressive and his speech contemptible'" (2 Corinthians 10:10). Ouch! Those are low blows. Apparently his accusers were not even bothering to be diplomatic about their criticism of his weaknesses.

How can an apostle admit to being lousy as a public speaker? Actually, fairly straightforwardly. "But even if I am unskilled in speech, yet I am not so in knowledge" (11:6). Paul admits the weakness. No smoke and mirrors, no rationalizations, just the truth. "It's true," Paul said. "I'm not a good speaker." Now for some of us that doesn't seem like much of an issue, but it would be like someone applying for an Internet technology job admitting that they can't seem to work well with this newfangled computer thing. In Paul's day, eloquence of speech was important, especially when communicating ideas of philosophy and religion.

Admitting a weakness can create a glass ceiling that can hold us back or give others something to use against us.

Because We Are Passionate About This Area

I still remember the feeling I had when I was told that I might not have the stuff it took to be a church planter. It was even more painful than the discussion I'd had a few years earlier with two pastors who told me they didn't think I'd ever make it as a pastor. (At this point, you're probably wondering how I became a pastor at all!) All I had ever wanted to do since I was fourteen years old was to be a pastor. I had no plan B. This goal consumed my life. It had driven me to complete eight years of biblical studies, working fulltime as a paperhanger to pay the bills. To say it was my passion would be an understatement. If you took the idea of being a pastor out of my future, I had none. How would I start over?

Now I need to point out something here. None of these guys were bad guys; they were good and godly men, but they had a certain idea of what it took to be a pastor and a church planter. I didn't fit that mold. It was a simple equation that required A plus B, and in their minds my weaknesses disqualified me. They were not trying to discourage me; they were actually trying to help me. I did have weaknesses (I still do), and these men believed they might cause me problems in my ministry.

They were right. I did have problems based on some of the issues they raised. But they were also wrong. God did amazing things through those very weaknesses, and when He did, He got the glory.

For the record, I did start the church, and over twenty-five years later it is alive and well. After thirteen years I moved on from that church and took another pastorate, where I have been for eleven years. But the bottom line is that after that I hesitated to admit any pastoral weaknesses for fear that my dream, my passion, might be imperiled by the admission.

Fear can be a powerful motivator for us to keep certain information about our weaknesses quiet, especially if that information might imperil our greatest passion.

Because We've Received Special Training in This Area

Face it! It's hard to admit our weakness if it's in an area where we have received special training. For example, every single pastor who went to seminary has been taught the subject of homiletics—the study of preaching. However, many pastors are not good at preaching. Special training does not make our weaknesses vanish, even if the training is in the area of our specific weakness.

Not every lawyer that passes the bar is immediately a good lawyer. Some will never be good lawyers, despite having all the training possible. A professor who is hired to teach may be absolutely abysmal at it. A person who has received training as a psychiatrist or psychologist may still have the people skills of Atilla the Hun. A person who has been trained in management may make a lousy manager, and a dietician may be overweight and unhealthy.

Sometimes the greatest obstacle to admitting our weakness is our own experience and training. We like to pad our resume and assure ourselves and everyone else that we are competent because, after all, we've got all this experience and training.

Paul didn't do that. To the Philippian church, he makes a great confession: "[I] put no confidence in the flesh" (Philippians

3:3). By "flesh" he doesn't mean the body; he means his human pedigree and accomplishments. He goes on to share specifics (3:4–6) so that the Philippians will know what he *doesn't* place confidence in:

He was circumcised on the eighth day, of the nation of Israel (his nationality).

He was of the tribe of Benjamin, a Hebrew of Hebrews (his family tree).

He was a Pharisee (the conservative religious party).

He was zealous (read energetic, ambitious, and driven).

He was blameless regarding the law (everyone knew he kept it).

Paul not only had special advantages that not every Hebrew had, he had also accomplished more than most. His training had been second to none. Then, one day, he took all those accomplishments, pedigrees, and his reputation and put them in the "loss" or "useless" column of his life. He no longer saw them as important; in fact, he describes them as "rubbish" (3:7–8). He replaced them all with the knowledge that he would now be able to "know [Christ] and the power of His resurrection and the fellowship of His sufferings" (3:10).

All the special training, advantages, and accomplishments in the world will not enable you to experience the power of Christ's resurrection in your life. Even though that is true, it is still difficult for us to admit a weakness in those areas where we've received special training. As a result, we continue to plod on, accomplishing little, growing more discouraged day after day.

Because We're Afraid We'll No Longer Be Useful

If I go around admitting my weaknesses—to myself or to others—I'm afraid that others with greater strengths will be used and I'll be sidelined. That is, until I remember how God works: "God has chosen the foolish things of the world to shame the wise, and God has chosen the weak things of the world to shame the things which are strong" (1 Corinthians 1:27). He consistently uses weak things to demonstrate His power, and we are some of the weak things He uses.

In her book *My Heart Sings*, Joni Eareckson Tada recalls a lunch she once enjoyed with Corrie ten Boom, a survivor of German concentration camps, speaker, and the author of *The Hiding Place*, now an elderly woman. Both women were confined to wheelchairs (Corrie now paralyzed by a stroke), both physically helpless.

> I relive each moment of my visit with Corrie ten Boom. I recall how our eyes met as we were fed our cucumber sandwiches. Helpless and for the most part dependent, I felt our mutual weakness. Yet I am certain neither of us had ever felt stronger. It makes me think of the Cross of Christ—a symbol of weakness and humiliation, yet at the same time, a symbol of victory and strength . . . For a wheelchair may confine a body that is wasting away. But no wheelchair can confine the soul . . . the soul that is inwardly renewed day by day. For paralyzed people can walk with the Lord. Speechless people can talk with the Almighty. Sightless people can see Jesus. Deaf people can hear the Word of God. And those like Tante Corrie, their minds shadowy and obscure, can have the very mind of Christ.[3]

Corrie and Joni have been two of the most influential and powerful women in the church in the last fifty years. The combined testimonies of these noteworthy women who have accomplished so much during their ministries and lives are a poignant reminder that God does not need healthy bodies or convenient circumstances to display His power. From a concentration camp in Germany and a quadriplegic's wheelchair God again reminds us that He "has chosen the weak things of the world to shame the things which are strong."

What weakness are we afraid will render us no longer useful? Is it a bad experience in our past? Does it compare with a German concentration camp? What is our physical weakness? Is it worse than losing the use of your arms and legs? God is showing over and over that He does not need our strength to display His power.

Because We Think God Wants Us to Feel Strong

This is most often a result of misunderstanding a very popular verse: "I can do all things through Him who strengthens me" (Philippians 4:13). We tend to focus on the "I can do all things" part, not the "through Him who strengthens me." I suppose it is the "can do" American spirit that attracts us to the first part and is confused by the second. Along with this is the idea that since we're Christians, we ought to be stronger than the average person. We have God on our side, and the Bible, and church.

Yet the only time Paul said "I am strong" was right after he said "for when I am weak." We may not feel weak, and we may not look weak, which is often our greatest problem. When all of our successes are easily explained by pointing to our training, methodology, talents, and circumstances, the results are weak precisely because they do not demonstrate clearly the power of God.

It is always amazing to me how good powerlessness can look.

We can operate in powerless mode for a very long time. Our results are acceptable to most—but if we were honest, we'd admit to disillusionment. With all the pluses we had going for us, we expected far more. Then we see someone who doesn't have nearly our I.Q., talents, opportunities, or experiences, but works of power are happening through them. Furthermore, we see God opening door after door for them.

When the results are unexpected and unexplainable given the circumstances, then we are witnessing the power of God. He loves to display His power through the weak: the weak prophet, the weak man or woman, the weak husband or wife, the weak parent or child, the weak student, employee, speaker, shepherd, the weak _____ (you fill in the blank). Sadly, we rarely give Him the opportunity to do just that.

We really believe that we are primed for success in many areas, and as a result we only ask (sincerely and genuinely) for help in those areas where we feel weak or inadequate. The truth is that we are *totally* weak and inadequate but don't know it. We often think God is waiting until we are strong enough for Him to use us. The clear and unequivocal teaching of Scripture is exactly the opposite. God is not waiting for us to become strong, but to admit our weakness, ask for His power, and watch Him work.

> Do you not know? Have you not heard?
> The Everlasting God, the LORD, the Creator of the ends of
>   the earth
> Does not become weary or tired.
> His understanding is inscrutable.

He gives strength to the weary,
And to him who lacks might He increases power.
Though youths grow weary and tired,
And vigorous young men stumble badly,
Yet those who wait for the LORD
Will gain new strength;
They will mount up with wings like eagles,
They will run and not get tired,
They will walk and not become weary" (Isaiah 40:28–31).

Because We Feel Safer Trusting in Ourselves

This has been a perennial problem for God's people down through the ages—and one of the main reasons people shy away from God and a relationship with Him. We have a problem trusting God. It's that simple. We don't like being weak, feeling weak, appearing weak, or admitting weakness. We much prefer feeling strong, appearing strong, and telling others how strong we are.

Paul pointed out (rather sarcastically) how these two ideologies were in conflict in Corinth where people were impressed with strength and honor. "We are fools for Christ's sake, but you are prudent in Christ; we are weak, but you are strong; you are distinguished, but we are without honor" (1 Corinthians 4:10).

British pastor and scholar N. T. Wright states, "We live in a world full of people struggling to be, or at least to appear strong, in order not to be weak; and we follow a gospel which says that when I am weak, then I am strong. And the gospel is the only thing that brings healing."[4]

Paul reminded the Ephesian Christians, "Finally, be strong in the Lord and in the strength of His might" (Ephesians 6:10).

Be strong, yes; but be strong in the Lord and in the strength of His might! Why did Paul have to keep bringing this up to church after church? Because it's such a hard lesson for us to learn.

The Lord through the prophet Isaiah issued a warning to Israel in the days when they were not interested in trusting in Him, when they felt they could get the help they needed from a foreign power. "Woe to those who go down to Egypt for help and rely on horses, and trust in chariots because they are many and in horsemen because they are very strong, but they do not look to the Holy One of Israel, nor seek the LORD!" (Isaiah 31:1).

Put simply, Israel felt safer trusting in their own ability to handle the problem than in God. They felt safer lining up armies with chariots and strong soldiers. I'd love to criticize them, but frankly, I'm too much like them to throw stones.

We'd rather not have to admit our weaknesses and ask for God's help; we'd rather just fix the problem ourselves. But there is one final reason why we are afraid to admit our weaknesses.

Because We Have Yet to See God Demonstrate His Power Through Our Weakness

We will deal with this more in another chapter, but we need to mention it here. We are afraid to admit our weakness because we haven't yet experienced the power of God through our weaknesses. Or, when we did we didn't recognize it as such. Since we aren't really sure what the power of God looks like or aren't used to seeing Him work in our lives, we can miss it. Too often when God does something amazing we just feel really lucky or fortunate.

But for Paul, the demonstration of God's power in his life wasn't an occasional option, it was his constant lifeline. In his second letter to the Corinthians, Paul shared some of his troubles—and his hope. "We do not want you to be unaware, brethren, of our affliction which came to us in Asia, that we were burdened excessively, beyond our strength, so that we despaired even of life; indeed, we had the sentence of death within ourselves so that we would not trust in ourselves, but in God who raises the dead; who delivered us from so great a peril of death, and will deliver us, He on whom we have set our hope. And He will yet deliver us" (2 Corinthians 1:8–10).

Paul's experiences were real, and his ability to depend on God's power for his life was now habitual. This is important for us to understand, because learning to depend on God's power through our weaknesses is not meant to be an option in our lives, but the way we face everything.

Paul makes the point more eloquently than I can in this passage, where he is defending himself against the false prophets. Read slowly and carefully and then ask yourself how someone could survive this kind of a life.

Are they servants of Christ?—I speak as if insane—I more so; in far more labors, in far more imprisonments, beaten times without number, often in danger of death. Five times I received from the Jews thirty-nine lashes. Three times I was beaten with rods, once I was stoned, three times I was shipwrecked, a night and a day I have spent in the deep. I have been on frequent journeys, in dangers from rivers, dangers from robbers, dangers from my countrymen, dangers from the Gentiles, dangers in the city, dangers in the wilderness, dangers on the sea, dangers among false brethren; I have been in labor and hardship, through many sleepless nights, in hunger and thirst, often without food, in cold and exposure. Apart from such external things, there is the daily pressure on me of concern for all the churches. Who is weak without my being weak? Who is led into sin without my intense concern? (2 Corinthians 11:23–29).

Do you remember the verse we started this chapter with? After sharing this overview of the terrible suffering and difficulty he had to endure, Paul shares this thought: "If I have to boast, I will boast of what pertains to my weakness" (2 Corinthians 11:30). It suddenly makes this short sentence far more powerful, doesn't it?

Doug Nichols shares the following story of finding power through weakness. It is instructive because, like us, Doug was not expecting what God was going to do.

While serving with Operation Mobilization in India in 1967, tuberculosis forced me into a sanitarium for several months. I did not yet speak the language, but I tried to give Christian literature written in their language to the patients, doctors, and nurses. Everyone politely refused. I sensed many weren't happy about a rich American (to them all Americans are rich) being in a free, government-run sanitarium. (They didn't know I was just as broke as they were!)

The first few nights I woke around 2:00 a.m. coughing. One morning during my coughing spell, I noticed one of the older and sicker patients across the aisle trying to get out of bed. He would sit up on the edge of the bed and try to stand, but in weakness would fall back into bed. I didn't understand what he was trying to do. He finally fell back into bed exhausted. I heard him crying softly.

The next morning I realized what the man had been trying to do. He had been trying to get up and walk to the bathroom! The stench in our ward was awful. Other patients yelled insults at the man. Angry nurses moved him roughly from side to side as they cleaned up the mess. One nurse even slapped him. The old man curled into a ball and wept. The next night I again woke up coughing. I noticed the man across the aisle sit up and again try to stand. Like the night before, he fell back whimpering.

I don't like bad smells, and I didn't want to become involved, but I got out of my bed and went over to him. When I touched his shoulder, his eyes opened wide with fear. I smiled, put my arms under him, and picked him up. He was very light due to old age and advanced TB. I carried him to the washroom, which was just a filthy, small room with a hole in the floor. I stood behind him with my arms under his armpits as he took care of himself. After he finished, I picked him up, and carried him back to his bed. As I laid him down, he kissed me on the cheek, smiled, and said something I couldn't understand.

The next morning another patient woke me and handed me a steaming cup of tea. He motioned with his hands that he wanted a tract. As the sun rose, other patients approached and indicated they also wanted the booklets I had tried to distribute before. Throughout my day nurses, interns, and doctors asked for literature. Weeks later an evangelist who spoke the language visited me, and as he talked to others he discovered that several had put their trust in Christ as Savior as a result of reading the literature. What did it take to reach these people with the gospel? It wasn't health, the ability to speak the language, or a persuasive talk. I simply took a trip to the bathroom.[5]

Our fear of admitting weakness is real, but so is the power of God available to us through that very same weakness. Perhaps at this point it would be best if we took a good long look at the power of God. We're far more likely to be willing to admit to weaknesses if we know what God wants to do through them. What is God's power, and what does it look like?

Let's find out.

CHAPTER FOUR

Recognizing God's Power

Natural strength is often as great a handicap as natural weakness. —HANNAH HURNARD

Harry Houdini, the great escape artist, became famous by escaping handcuffs, prison cells, and all manner of contraptions designed to confine him. He boasted on numerous occasions that no jail cell could hold him. Then he would visit a city and claim he could escape their jail cell. He never failed. He always escaped.

Well, almost always.

The story is told that on one particular occasion Harry entered a cell as he usually did, wearing his street clothes. The authorities shut the jail cell behind him and left him. Alone, he did what he had done so many times before: he pulled a thin but strong piece of metal from his belt and began working the lock. But this time the cell wouldn't open. The lock would not yield. He worked feverishly, applying his amazing knowledge of locks and their mechanisms to the task. Two hours later, in frustration and failure, he gave up. The lock simply would not yield. The Great Houdini had finally failed.

What was the problem? What went wrong?

The guards had forgotten to lock the cell!

All he ever needed to do was push open the cell door. The only place the door was locked was in Houdini's mind.

Now, think of those who are trying so hard to appropriate the power of God for their everyday lives, seeking method after method for unleashing God's power but never quite able to pick the lock behind which the power of God must surely reside. Finally, they quit in frustration, assuming that somehow the power they seek is just too elusive or meant for some select few or people in the distant past. But the power is there; we're just looking in the wrong place.

Philip Yancey, in his book *Reaching for the Invisible God*, writes, "People expect power from their God, not powerlessness, strength not weakness, largeness not smallness."[1]

It is no small thing for the average disciples of Jesus to admit that they do not experience the power of God in their lives. It is, in a way, humiliating. Yes, we believe we are sons and daughters of God and that He has promised us power to live our lives—but for some reason the power doesn't come. We feel just as weak and powerless as we ever have. Maybe we don't have enough faith, we surmise. And that is, perhaps, even more depressing than the thought that God has promised power we can't access.

It's like buying a new car with air conditioning and discovering that you have no way to turn it on.

You feel helpless and hopeless.

The Hope We Need to Revive

William Barclay wrote, "The Christian hope is the hope which has seen everything and endured everything, and has still not despaired, because it believes in God. The Christian hope is not hope in the human spirit, in human goodness, in human endurance, in human achievement; the Christian hope is hope in the power of God."[2]

This is the hope that we need to revive.

Promises of power are woven inextricably through the entire New Testament, reminding us of the resource God has provided for every Christian to live victoriously. But before we can begin to talk in depth about seeing God's power in our lives, we must first determine what the power of God really is.

As we do that, we must be aware that many of our human ideas about power will do little more than confuse us. These ideas deal almost exclusively with physical strength, physical resources, or demonstrations of explosive power, along with muscle competitions, martial arts exhibitions, weapons of mass destruction, economic power, and other powers that can be exerted to force one will upon another. Modern scientific knowledge and technology is another form of human power that awes us. It is the power in some form to intimidate or impress, whether it's a bully flexing his muscles, a professor flexing her knowledge, or a businessman flexing his wallet.

God's power has often been misunderstood because we tend to think of it in just those terms: physical strength, omniscient knowledge, or a wealth of resources at His disposal. This is where we often get skeptics asking questions like "Can God make a rock so big that He can't pick it up?" This is an example of confusing the attribute of omnipotence (possessing all power) that belongs to God alone with human strength—in other words, seeing His attribute in simply human terms. But omnipotence is nothing like that.

The power of God is demonstrated by His ability to accomplish His will in every situation, both real and potential, through any means He chooses in order to glorify himself. The attribute of omnipotence is simply the power to execute His will. As theologian Henry Thiessen writes, "He is able to do whatever He will; but since His will is limited by His nature, this means that God can do *everything that is in harmony with His perfections.*"[3]

This answers the question, "Can God make a rock so big that He can't pick it up?" God is a unified being who does not exercise one of His attributes at the expense of another. His omniscience (all knowingness) informs His omnipotence. He is a unified being, without contradiction. And this reminds us that, because of His attributes, there are some things that God *cannot* do.

God cannot lie (Numbers 23:19; 1 Samuel 15:29). Since this is true, His promise to give us power to live the Christian life must be true.

God cannot sin (James 1:13; Habakkuk 1:13). He will not pull a bait and switch on us, promising us power and then intentionally withholding it for unknown reasons. God is not a deceiver.

God cannot deny himself (2 Timothy 2:13). God is faithful to His nature and promises.

The Bible gives many examples and evidences of God's power, and as we look at them we will see that His power is so much greater than we thought it was and is seen in ways we could never have imagined.

Evidences of God's Power

His Creative Power

By faith we understand that the worlds were prepared by the word of God, *so that what is seen was not made out of things which are visible* (Hebrews 11:3).

By the word of the LORD the heavens were made, and by the breath of His mouth all their host . . . *for He spoke, and it was done*; He commanded, and it stood fast (Psalm 33:6, 9).

In our human world people get excited about the concept of "creating life" and assure themselves that if/when it happens, it will be perhaps the greatest display of human power. Occasionally we read a journalist breathlessly reporting that a scientist somewhere is close to doing just that. But the fact is that with all our modern scientific and technological superiority, we can't make so much as a piece of lint *out of nothing*—not if we tried for the next 50,000 years. We can manipulate the elements we have been given, but we cannot create them. The creative power of God to speak into existence the world we inhabit and explore—out of nothing—demonstrates His unique and unfathomable power.

Too often when we think of God's power, we understand it in some limited way because, despite what we've read in Scripture, that's the only way we've really seen it. We know about what God has done in the past, and that impresses us, but it doesn't always translate into trust in our lives. In fact, those stories simply make us nostalgic for the "good old days" when everyone got to see God send plagues, part the Red Sea, create a worldwide flood, and more. It can seem as if God doesn't exercise His power in our world very often anymore, at least not in ways we can see.

His Supernatural Power

We are all familiar with smoke and mirrors—the tricks that the famous illusionists of our day use to make the impossible look possible. But they have to do this in very controlled situations, with proper lighting, mirrors, and misdirection. God's power has been displayed throughout the ages in situations in which there was no controlling for angles, not nearly enough smoke, and mirrors were often not even available.

When God used Moses to turn the Nile into blood, everyone could see that it was real—no tricks. When God made the sun stand still for Joshua, the world could see it. When Jesus walked on the water, turned water into wine, raised Lazarus from the dead, healed people of organic diseases, fed the five thousand with a few loaves and fish, calmed the storm with a word, there were people there to see these miracles.

"Some see miracles as an implausible suspension of the laws of the physical universe," says author and speaker Philip Yancey. "As signs, though, they serve just the opposite function. Death, decay, entropy, and destruction are the true suspensions of God's laws; miracles are the early glimpses of restoration. In the words of Jurgen Moltman, 'Jesus' healings are not supernatural miracles in a natural world. They are the only true "natural" things in a world that is unnatural, demonized and wounded.'"[4]

His Transformative Power

From the radical conversion of the Christian-hating-and-murdering Saul of Tarsus, who later became the beloved apostle Paul, to James the brother of Jesus who was skeptical of his sibling, the power of God has been evidenced in changing people's entire lives. As a student of human nature, I can assure you that one of the most difficult things in the entire world is to change every part of your life, your values, your direction, your outlook, your prejudices, your goals. Yet the power of God through the gospel, through His Spirit has been doing that for thousands of years.

How much success would a gospel of a God becoming a man and living a sinless human life, then dying for the sins of the whole world have on a culture steeped in paganism? Listen to Paul's greetings and encouragement to the church at Thessalonica:

> For they themselves report about us what kind of a reception we had with you, and how you turned to God from idols to serve a living and true God, and to wait for His Son from heaven, whom He raised from the dead, that is Jesus, who rescues us from the wrath to come (1 Thessalonians 1:9–10).

What about C. S. Lewis, the brilliant scholar and avowed atheist who finally came to Christ through the power of this gospel? Or Lee Strobel, the award-winning journalist and atheist who finally came to faith in Christ? What of Chuck Colson, the ex-Nixon hatchet man? We could go on and on, citing people we have heard of or people we know personally who were as far away from God as they could get, but who now can testify of how God's power changed their hearts first, their lives second.

The New Testament is itself an anthology of change—change in people and ultimately change in culture. It didn't begin with powerful people. None of the early Christians were powerful. They were also very unpopular, persecuted, and maligned. Yet because of their influence, within three hundred years the Roman Empire had become a Christian empire. If we don't see the power of God here, we are missing it in one of its greatest forms. It takes an unimaginable power to change a person who is unwilling to change, resistant to change, or even hostile to change. The power of God poured out on the human heart is an amazing thing to watch.

His Power to Accomplish His Perfect Will

The Bible is replete with stories of how God influenced events to accomplish His perfect will. Biblical prophecy is a shining example of that. God not only knows what is going to happen in the future; His power makes it happen. He influenced Pharaoh to have dreams that required Joseph to interpret them, which led to Joseph's influential role in Egypt. He used King Ahasuerus's discontent with his wife to seek another, which led to his choosing Esther; she and her Uncle Mordecai were then used to deliver the Jewish people from mass genocide in Persia. He "stirred up the spirit" of King Cyrus of Persia to send the Hebrews back to their land, back to Jerusalem to rebuild the temple.

He caused a census to be taken of the whole world in the days of Roman Emperor Augustus Caesar which brought Joseph and Mary back to their hometown of Bethlehem where the Messiah was born, thus fulfilling prophecy. He caused disturbances in the heavens which led wise men from the East to come and find the reason for it all, following a star the whole way.

We could go on and on, book by book in the Bible to show the power of God to influence events to accomplish His objective every time, despite sometimes overwhelming obstacles.

His Power to Protect and Enable His People to Do the Impossible

Shadrach, Meshach, and Abednego were three Hebrews who refused to bow down to the golden image of King Nebuchadnezzar of Babylon. Their punishment was to be thrown into a fiery furnace. They not only survived but were walking around within the fire, and when called out by Nebuchadnezzar, they did not even have the smell of smoke upon them.

Daniel was not born with the ability to interpret dreams,

but when the time came and the need arose, God displayed His power in giving Daniel an ability that was not innate. All the wise men of the day that Nebuchadnezzar had relied on to interpret his dreams had failed. Daniel exceeded them all with his ability to interpret the king's dreams because God displayed His power through him.

How did Peter walk on water with Jesus? Against every law of nature we know, Peter walked on a liquid for a period of time until his faith faltered. Every one of the apostles of Christ was able to do miracles, supernatural events, through the power of Christ in them.

How did the apostles in the book of Acts speak in tongues, even dialects of foreign languages they had never learned? It wasn't some crash course in linguistics that accomplished this, simultaneously, for all the disciples. It was the power of God!

Resurrection!

There is no greater display of power than to bring someone back to life who has breathed his last and been buried for four days, as Jesus did with Lazarus. And only the power of God could resurrect Jesus after His death and burial in the tomb for three days—restored not only to life, but glorious eternal life. Doctors can resuscitate a person who has stopped breathing or whose heart has stopped beating and is clinically dead, but that has to be done immediately. After a person has been dead for three days (or even an hour), we have no power to regenerate life. Only God has that power, and it is the Christian's great hope and joy. Because our God has this power, we will live forever in new glorified bodies, even though our old bodies have died and decayed on the earth.

God's power, as we have seen, is shown in a variety of

different ways. His creative power, His supernatural power, His transformative power to change lives dramatically and permanently, His ability to influence events to accomplish His perfect will, His power to protect and enable His people to do the impossible, and His power to resurrect people from the dead are all ways God displays His power in our world.

But this is not just in the past. God is still a creative God (read Revelation 21 and 22 about the new heaven and the new earth He plans to create). He still works supernaturally, demonstrating His power over and through nature. He still changes lives dramatically and permanently, and He still influences events to accomplish what we never could on our own. And every time a believer's body dies, there is another resurrection into eternal life.

Power Comes from God

So why aren't we seeing and experiencing more of God's power in our own lives? One important reason is that the power of God comes *from* God. Any hope of keeping God at arm's length or ignoring His will for our lives and still experiencing His power is misplaced. *God uses His power on our behalf to accomplish His perfect will.* If we are honest, we are not always open to that particular option. We say we are, but are we really?

God will not provide His power to accomplish anything that is not in His perfect will. Though He had the power, our Lord did not call down ten thousand angels to stop His crucifixion, for that crucifixion was in the will of His Father for Him.

Most of us have our lives mapped out—how and where we want to live, what we want to do, how much we want to earn, the lifestyle we want to enjoy, the kind of person we want to marry. The power of God is not some faceless, formless force we can somehow appropriate to carry out our wishes. If we are not interested in seeking God's will for our lives, seeking His power is a waste of time. The case of Simon in the book of Acts reminds us of that truth (Acts 8:9–24).

Do you think God would have agreed if Moses had asked for a couple more miracles to cement his own legacy in Israel? Not likely. You don't order God's power in your life like a book on Amazon.com. His power is ultimately a reflection of His will, so seeking His power in our lives is really seeking His perfect will for our lives—asking Him to intervene in powerful ways when we encounter obstacles to accomplishing His will. What we often do instead is ask God to *give us* power, or *make us* strong—and what we really mean is that we want Him to give us an emotional feeling of invincibility to achieve our plans or goals, or to divinely manipulate circumstances and people to make them favorable to our goals.

God's power always has a holy and perfect purpose. He cannot be bamboozled into meaningless displays of power. When the Jews demanded a sign from Jesus, He refused (Matthew 12:38–42). God wants to demonstrate His power on our behalf, in view of our weaknesses, with the purpose of accomplishing His will. He wants to show His power through our weaknesses, not remove our weaknesses and replace them with strength. Paul learned that lesson with his thorn in the flesh.

If God suddenly made us feel powerful, or if He just removed our weaknesses and altered all our negative circumstances, would we sense our continuing need of His presence and power in our lives? Would we become more or less dependent upon Him? And how long would it take before we forgot where the power and strength we suddenly acquired came from? When God gave Solomon wisdom so that he was "wiser than all men" (1 Kings 4:29–34), did Solomon become more dependent upon God or did he begin to feel and walk and live independent of God? His story is instructive (see 1 Kings 11).

Your Greatest Weakness Is God's Gateway

Human weakness is the perfect opportunity for God to demonstrate His power to accomplish anything that is in His perfect will. Your greatest weakness can become the gateway to God's greatest demonstration of power in your life.

Was God just picking on Paul when he asked God to remove his physical weaknesses and God said, "My grace is sufficient for you, for power is perfected in weakness" (2 Corinthians 12:9)? Was Paul to be the only one who would be able to say, "When I am weak, then I am strong" (12:10)?

When Peter talks about serving "by the strength which God supplies; so that in all things God may be glorified through Jesus Christ" (1 Peter 4:11), what does he mean?

When Jesus said our flesh is weak, what did He mean (Mark 14:38)? What are the present-day implications?

What is the meaning behind the words of Isaiah the prophet when he warns Israel not to go down to Egypt for help and rely on their soldiers and their horses (Isaiah 31:1)?

It's not that the power of God is complicated or that how we appropriate it is complicated. It is that *we* are complicated. Many of us say things we don't really believe and confess things we don't really practice. Yet I believe that true disciples of Jesus want to be changed, want to experience His power in their lives, so the answer must lie somewhere in our understanding of our need for it and how to appropriate it.

If you ask Christians whether they believe God is all-powerful, most will quickly say "Yes!" If you ask if they believe God can do anything (consistent with His nature and being), they will enthusiastically agree. If you then press them and ask if God can powerfully change their lives, they will probably say "Yes," but at this point they may be giving you nervous looks. And if you then ask if they think God *can change their lives powerfully and dramatically,* you will at the very least get some hesitation, and most likely a non-committal shrug. Our theology and doctrine may be right, but our past experiences can get in the way.

God's power *always* has a holy and perfect purpose. He cannot be bamboozled into meaningless displays of power. In short, God will not provide His power to accomplish anything that will not glorify himself. So if He will not display His power apart from His perfect will, we need to know what His good and perfect will is for every believer, because that will affect all equally.

CHAPTER FIVE

Discovering God's Power Points

God . . . is not in the business of helping the humanly strong become stronger; rather he takes the weak and makes them strong in himself. —ERWIN LUTZER

In the movie *National Treasure*, the main character, Benjamin Franklin Gates, has been obsessed since he was a boy with finding the legendary Knights Templar treasure, the greatest fortune known to man. To find that elusive treasure, Gates constantly has to decipher a seemingly never-ending set of clues and riddles. Each time he deciphers a clue, he feels he is on the verge of finding the treasure, only to be disappointed. He is rewarded with another clue, which leads him to another clue, and on and on it goes.

For many Christians this seems to be how we find God's will for our lives. We can never really know what He wants us to do because He never comes right out and tells us. Yet when most Christians talk about finding the will of God for their lives, what they are really talking about are those secret things of the future: Who should I marry? Where should I go to school? What vocation should I pursue? Should I get the surgery or not? Is this a wise investment? We want to solve the mystery of what our future is going to look like.

Yet to speak of the will of God for our lives as a mystery is a great mistake. What God wants for us—for each of us—is no mystery. God never intended to make His will for us like a treasure hunt that requires a secret map or hidden clues. On the contrary, He left us a clear set of instructions, found over and over again in the Bible.

If we are seeking God's power in our lives, it behooves us to first determine that for which He has promised to give us power. There are so many wonderful things for which God has promised to give us His power that we would indeed be foolish if we failed to focus on them. The greatest of these is quite often not even on our radar, yet it is the purpose for which we were created.

To Glorify God

It is God's will for every person who has ever lived or will ever live and for all of creation to glorify Him. Everything that was made was made for the glory of God.

The heavens are telling of the glory of God; and their expanse is declaring the work of His hands. Day to day pours forth speech, and night to night reveals knowledge. There is no speech, nor are there words; their voice is not heard (Psalm 19:1–3).

For from Him and through Him and to Him are all things. To Him be the glory forever. Amen (Romans 11:36).

For by Him all things were created, both in the heavens and on earth, visible and invisible, whether thrones or dominions or rulers or authorities—all things have been created through Him and for Him (Colossians 1:16).

And when the living creatures give glory and honor and thanks to Him who sits on the throne, to Him who lives forever and ever, the twenty-four elders will fall down before Him who sits on the throne, and will worship Him who lives forever and ever, and will cast their crowns before the throne, saying, "Worthy are You, our Lord and our God, to receive glory and honor and power; for You created all things, and because of Your will they existed, and were created" (Revelation 4:9–11).

The Westminster Shorter Catechism reminds us that "Man's chief end is to glorify God, and to enjoy him forever." If we are tempted to say that this seems a rather proud, demanding, and self-serving sort of command from God, we need to remember that we're talking about God. In a man or woman it would indeed be proud, demanding, and self-serving, because we would, in effect, be seeking to glorify sinful imperfection. To glorify sinful imperfection is sin. But God is absolutely sinless and perfect in holiness; He is the *only* One who is like this. For Him to seek His own glory is for Him to seek to glorify absolute holiness and sinless perfection. In short, there is nothing and no one higher to glorify than God.

Pastor and author Max Lucado once said, "There is a canyon of difference between doing your best to glorify God and doing whatever it takes to glorify yourself. The quest for excellence is a mark of maturity. The quest for power is childish."[1] To seek personal power for ourselves is an unworthy goal, but to seek His power to glorify Him in our lives is a mark of spiritual maturity.

Everything God created, including us, was designed to declare His glory, and every other aspect of God's will flows out of this great and divine purpose. Let's look at some of those.

Our Personal Holiness

How many times have you tried to stop a particular sin or sinful attitude or habit and failed? We desperately want to change, and we despair over the feelings of guilt and shame that accompany our failures. It sometimes seems that we take three steps forward and two steps back. And yet it is God's will for us to be holy.

> For I am the LORD who brought you up from the land of Egypt to be your God; thus *you shall be holy, for I am holy* (Leviticus 11:45).

> *Thus you are to be holy to Me, for I the LORD am holy;* and I have set you apart from the peoples to be Mine (Leviticus 20:26).

> Blessed be the God and Father of our Lord Jesus Christ, who has blessed us with every spiritual blessing in the heavenly places in Christ, *just as He chose us in Him before the foundation of the world, that we would be holy and blameless before Him* (Ephesians 1:3–4).

> As obedient children, do not be conformed to the former lusts which were yours in your ignorance, but *like the Holy One who called you, be holy yourselves also in all your behavior; because it is written, "YOU SHALL BE HOLY, FOR I AM HOLY"* (1 Peter 1:14–16).

Holiness means that we turn away from the sinful impulses and desires that so ensnared and ruled us before we came to know Christ, and we ask Him to replace those desires with His desires and thoughts. It's not simply the ability to resist temptation; it is a change of desire within our heart and mind. A holy people are not simply a people who "don't" commit this or that sin, but a people who *don't want to* anymore. Their actions have changed because their desires have changed.

Given all of this, does it not make sense that God would want His power in our lives to give us victory over sin? Isn't this one of the truly great and tangible results of the power of God in lives? Aren't we amazed when people whose lives were literally destroyed by sin suddenly and powerfully are transformed into holy people? And be honest, don't you wish you were like them?

How many Christians have felt they could not possibly be Christians because they have lost the battle against sin in their lives? The tragic thing is that they have memorized the truths of God, tried so hard to obey them, agonized, cried out in shame over their sins, but never seemed to have the power to change.

But take comfort in this: God desires your holiness and is willing to provide all the power you need to become holy. A. W. Tozer said, "Christianity takes for granted the absence of any self-help and offers a power which is nothing less than the power of God."

Attempts to marshal all our human resources (will power, intelligence, resolve) to help us be holy are doomed to failure (you've probably realized that by now). The Christian life, the life of holiness, can never be a natural life in a sin-infected world with a sin-infected nature, so it must require a supernatural power to achieve. To me, that is such a relief. Having failed so miserably on my own, I have watched in wonder and amazement as He has enabled me to live in holiness (not perfection) in the very areas that I struggled with so long. In such situations I "am well content with weakness," for His power is perfected in my weakness.

Power for Witness

So when they had come together, they were asking Him, saying, "Lord, is it at this time You are restoring the kingdom to Israel?" He said to them, "It is not for you to know times or epochs which the Father has fixed by His own authority; *but you will receive power when the Holy Spirit has come upon you; and you shall be My witnesses* both in Jerusalem, and in all Judea and Samaria, and even to the remotest part of the earth" (Acts 1:6–8).

In this familiar and disturbingly clear passage we are promised power to be His witnesses. I don't know how many times I have heard this passage preached at missions conferences or in sermons (I've done it myself quite a few times), but every time I hear it I squirm. The feeling that I experience most frequently when I think about sharing my faith is guilt. I never feel like I share enough or take advantage of the opportunities presented to me. Simply put, sharing my faith is not in my comfort zone.

Though I will be the first to admit that I am not gifted as an evangelist, I have seen God work through my weakness to bring people from the kingdom of darkness into the kingdom of light. Many times over the years I have had opportunities to share the gospel with someone, and I have led many people into a relationship with Jesus. And every time I have been nervous and felt powerless. Yet in my powerlessness, He has worked.

When you think about it, this is the greatest power-encounter in our world today. All the power of hell is set against it, and the power of the risen Christ is set toward it, and the result is that people are being set free from the power and dominion of the kingdom of Satan and entering the kingdom of God.

Jesus said that we would receive power, and I think for many years I felt Acts 1:8 should read, "And you will feel powerful when the Holy Spirit has come upon you, and thus it will be easy and natural for you to be my witnesses." When the feelings of power didn't come, I thought maybe I had an excuse to be absent. I was waiting for a feeling of certainty that God had never promised. Yet frequently in my uncertainty, and very often to my complete surprise, He used me to lead someone to Him. His power was obviously at work.

Think about what just one conversion to Christ entails, especially to someone who has rejected Him for any period of time. The basic foundations upon which they have built their life have to be destroyed and forsaken in order to receive Christ. What they have believed all their lives, what they have committed themselves to—ideas and thoughts they have held and even championed— have to be abandoned. Assumptions that have guided them their entire lives have to be rejected. They have to humble themselves completely before One greater than they could ever imagine. Nothing short of the power of Christ can accomplish this.

God wants to and will provide all the power we need to be His witnesses, and this is a great comfort to those, like me, who find it a bit intimidating.

Growing Faith

When He got into the boat, His disciples followed Him. And behold, there arose a great storm on the sea, so that the boat was being covered with the waves; but Jesus

Himself was asleep. And they came to Him and woke Him, saying, "Save us, Lord; we are perishing!" He said to them, "Why are you afraid, you men of little faith?" Then He got up and rebuked the winds and the sea, and it became perfectly calm. The men were amazed, and said, "What kind of a man is this, that even the winds and the sea obey Him?" (Matthew 8:23–27).

We read here and many other places in the Gospels that Jesus was disappointed in the level of faith of His disciples, especially in light of His works. It is clear that God wants our faith in Him to grow. He wants us to trust His character, His intentions, and His providential will for our lives. Ironically, these are often the things of which we are most frightened. We can't help worrying that His intentions and His will for our lives will bring nothing but heartache and problems, while our will and intentions for our lives will bring nothing but sunshine and smiles. This is a serious lack of faith in the character of our God—and a serious over-estimation of our own wisdom.

Our faith in God is strengthened when we unmistakably see His work in our lives. We recognize His work in someone else's life and are impressed. But when we begin to embrace our own weaknesses and seek His power for our lives in specific situations, the Lord honors His Word and we begin to see demonstrations of His power. Then our faith is strengthened as we see these works that are so demonstrably powerful and clear that we recognize them as His work. God wants our faith in Him to grow exponentially, and He is fully prepared to demonstrate His power to confirm our faith in both His character and His power. He wants us to live in an ever-increasing awareness of His intimate involvement in our lives.

We can with full confidence pursue an increasing faith in God through the workings of His power in our lives. "For we walk by faith, not by sight" (2 Corinthians 5:7).

Personal Transformation

One of the saddest things in the world is Christians who have convinced themselves that they will never change. Whether it is a particular sin, or a habit, or a dangerous or destructive attitude that lingers, or a lack of faith that cripples their Christian life, they are convinced that they will never change because—well, they've been working on it for years and they never have.

In a sense, of course, they are quite right. They won't or can't change apart from the power of God. That has always been true.

> Therefore I urge you, brethren, by the mercies of God, to present your bodies a living and holy sacrifice, acceptable to God, which is your spiritual service of worship. And do not be conformed to this world, but *be transformed by the renewing of your mind, so that you may prove what the will of God is*, that which is good and acceptable and perfect (Romans 12:1–2).

It couldn't be stated any clearer: God wants us to be transformed by the renewing of our minds. It is His will for us. All of us.

Knowing this makes it that much harder when we realize we are not seeing this in our lives to the extent we know we should. Wrong ideas, wrong thoughts, wrong actions need to be confronted with the truth of God in our lives and then transformed in us by the power of Christ. We need to seek out the truth of God that confronts our wrong ideas and attitudes, and through the Spirit of God's guidance we can. It is at this point that we often quit, however, highlighting again our cultural problem.

We see a problem. We see the solution. And we simply try to apply the solution to the problem. Unfortunately, the problem is much larger than we realize, and the solution we apply is much too weak to make any difference.

Old Faithful in Yellowstone National Park is a geothermal geyser that regularly builds up intensity and power underground and then seeks release through the blowhole, creating an amazing spectacle as it erupts. Now imagine that I find this blowing off of steam both embarrassing and destructive, so I apply a solution. I put a plastic pail over the blowhole to keep the geyser under control. The problem of course is that the pressure underground is far more powerful than the plastic pail's ability to stop its tremendous force. When the geyser erupts, it blows that pail hundreds of feet in the air.

Yet that's how many of us try to be transformed. Unaware of the incredible power of our sin nature, we try putting a series of spiritual pails over it to keep it under control, and they all fail abysmally. We try to overcome lust by staying away from lewd pictures. A pail. We try to overcome our anger and rage by counting to ten first. A pail. We try to curb our hateful thoughts toward someone by internalizing them instead of sharing them verbally. A pail.

They never work. They can't. The power of our sin nature is exponentially stronger than any pail we try to use. It will take nothing short of Christ's resurrection power in our lives to gain the victory. It is a task we cannot ever hope to handle by ourselves. But here's the rub: We have to really believe that. If we don't, we will forever be trying to put pails over the geyser of our sin nature.

Simply put, we don't have what it takes to do the job. If God doesn't help us, we're sunk. But because transformation is God's will for us, He will provide the power if we ask for it

Providential Direction

When we speak of providential direction—that is, seeking God's will for our lives—we struggle with applying the concept of power. Yet remember, God's power is directed toward doing whatever is necessary to accomplish *His will*.

God has called each one of us to do certain things—things He hasn't called all of us to do. There are billions of women in this world, yet God's will for me was to marry only one, Annette. It was God's will from that union to produce three children, Christi, Andrew, and Katie. It was His will that I become a pastor and move to Santa Ynez and pastor Shoreline Community Church.

God didn't post the position and schedule interviews for "leading God's people out of Egypt"; Moses was given that specific job. Jonah the prophet was called to preach repentance to the city of Nineveh. God didn't call anyone else to do that; it had to be Jonah. Jacob had twelve sons, yet it was only Joseph that God determined would be ruler over the other brothers and counselor to Pharaoh. Many Jews became Christians in the New Testament, but only Paul was called to be the apostle to the Gentiles. It was Philip who was led to meet and share the gospel with the Ethiopian eunuch. And we could go on and on citing biblical examples of providential direction.

God calls each one of us to strengthen His church, but each in a different way. Each one of us has a part in building His kingdom on earth, but each of us has a slightly different gift or ability or task. How can we know what it is? The power of God is available for just such situations. It is His will that we walk in His will; therefore we must be able to discern His will. Humanly, this is impossible. How can the finite understand the infinite? As Isaiah said,

> "For My thoughts are not your thoughts,
> Nor are your ways My ways," declares the LORD.
> "For as the heavens are higher than the earth,
> So are My ways higher than your ways
> And My thoughts than your thoughts" (Isaiah 55:8–9).

Where God has clearly explained His will for our lives in Scripture, we can know it. However, I looked in vain for the verse that said, "Dan, marry Annette; have three children and name them Christi, Andrew, and Katie; write books and articles; and pastor Shoreline Community Church." Nothing less than the amazing power of God is necessary to discern and follow His will for my specific life. Furthermore, I only get as much knowledge and leading as I need for the moment.

Though the ultimate destination of our lives is a mystery to us, God is committed to helping us discover the steps along the way: "Trust in the LORD with all your heart, and do not lean on your own understanding. In all your ways acknowledge Him, and *He will make your paths straight*" (Proverbs 3:5–6).

Recently we bought a new home after a long and difficult process. To begin with, we made a bid on a house we liked. We signed a contract, agreed on a price (higher than we wanted but we were willing to pay it), and waited for the bank to get back to us. And over a year later they finally did! The bank asked us if we still wanted to buy the house, and if we did, we'd better get going. So we did. Then we didn't hear from anyone for two more months. Annette and I wondered if this was truly God's will for us.

Then I discovered what had caused the problem. I did some research, went online, made a few calls, and fixed the problem. Then the bank came to us again and said, "Well, if you want to buy the house, you'd better make a bid on it." Seriously, I am not making this up. So we made a bid on the house (again), a bid that was *significantly less* than our previous bid—and they accepted.

Throughout all of this, that verse kept coming back to us: "Do not lean on your own understanding. In all your ways acknowledge Him and He will make your paths straight." When we grew frustrated about the lack of progress, we forgot about the house and simply did what God wanted us to do in other areas of life.

We realize now that because of the holdup in the process, we got the house for a much more affordable price, but there was no way we could have known or understood that at the time. The power of God! He led us step by step, never giving us more information than we absolutely needed. Things that looked like they would kill the deal actually ended up making the deal better. Only He controls all the circumstances of life!

Rarely do we feel as helpless and weak as when we are trying to discern the will of our God in the specific details of our lives. That feeling is healthy. How can we possibly discover and understand the will of an all-wise, all-knowing God for particular situations in our lives unless God himself intercedes for us? We need the power of God, nothing less.

Strength in Times of Difficulty and Weakness

There are those times in life when everything seems to be against us. All of our efforts to fix the problem have failed, solutions elude us, resources are unavailable, and we get one closed door after another. We become weary, beaten down, mentally worn-out, and emotionally drained. It seems like everything is stacked against us.

We're not sure we can face another day, and yet we see an unending number of days of difficulty ahead. In these moments, when we realize all our human resources have failed, we are most open to requesting the power of God. We know that only His intervention will rescue us.

And what is God's promise for us?

> Do you not know? Have you not heard? The Everlasting God, the LORD, the Creator of the ends of the earth does not become weary or tired. His understanding is inscrutable. He gives strength to the weary, *and to him who lacks might He increases power*. Though youths grow weary and tired, and vigorous young men stumble badly, yet *those who wait for the LORD will gain new strength*; they will mount up with wings like eagles, they will run and not get tired, they will walk and not become weary (Isaiah 40:28–31).

Unless you have experienced this weariness—this coming to the end of yourself—the prophet's words may sound like hyperbole or poetic wishful thinking. But to those who have experienced it, it is a precious promise of needed power. Few things are more freeing than the knowledge that at these times we do not need to try to find our own power or search deeper within ourselves for more strength.

John Claypool was an Episcopalian priest whose young daughter suffered from leukemia. When she went into remission, everybody thought that God had possibly healed her. On an Easter Sunday morning, however, she went into a terrible recurrence. In his book *Tracks of a Fellow Struggler*, Claypool relates how for two weeks his daughter was wracked with pain, her eyes swollen shut. She asked him, "Daddy, did you talk to God about my leukemia?"

He said, "Yes, dear, we've been praying for you."

"Did you ask him how long the leukemia would last? What did God say?"

What do you say to your daughter when you can't help her and the heavens are silent? Emotionally and spiritually he was exhausted. A few hours later, she died.

The following Sunday morning, John Claypool stepped into the pulpit to preach. His text was Isaiah 40:31: "Those who hope in the Lord will renew their strength. They will soar on wings like eagles; they will run and not grow weary, they will walk and not be faint" (NIV).

Dr. Claypool reminded his congregation that there are three stages of life. Sometimes we soar and fly like an eagle. We're on top of the world. Sometimes we run and don't grow weary. We just go through the routine. And sometimes it's all we can do to walk and not faint. Then he asked the congregation for their prayers and encouragement. In his lowest, his weakest moment, he preached perhaps his most influential sermon. It came at his darkest hour, and he could say, like Paul, "for when I am weak, then I am strong."[2]

To find strength in the midst of the worst imaginable circumstances is one of the greatest blessings available to a Christian. And that is what God promises for us—to bring to our lives precisely what we so desperately need, at the precise moment we most need it. His power can bring us His strength when our own fails us. I've experienced this truth so many times.

Hope in Times of Despair

This may seem very much like what we just talked about, yet hope is different than strength. God can give us strength to go on when we are weary; but strength to go on, to endure, is not the same as hope. Hope is light at the end of the tunnel, the belief that the horrible circumstances I'm experiencing now won't last—or maybe, more honestly, that I won't feel the same way I do about them now.

> Now may the God of hope fill you with all joy and peace in believing, *that you will abound in hope by the power of the Holy Spirit* (Romans 15:13).

Hope is something that God's power makes available to us, and "abounding in hope" comes about through the power of the Holy Spirit. The hope of the Christian is not a self-manufactured passion or emotion, or a last-ditch gasp for something to make everything better. Hope from God is God releasing to us something He has that we don't. In Him we find the source of hope for every situation. He is the light at the end of the tunnel, He is the light in the darkness, and He is the One who can create hope in us when nothing else can. He alone knows where we are supposed to be, what we are supposed to be doing, what we will need to do what He wants, and when we will need that help.

If someone were dying of cancer, if someone had just lost his job, if someone had just lost everything she had, would you know how to bring them hope? Neither would I. How often have you tried to bring hope to someone in difficult situations only to fail? Only God can plumb the depths of the soul and know the place where light needs to pierce darkness, where a new truth is needed to slay despair, where an old truth needs to be resurrected to bring hope to life again. Only God. Knowing us intimately, He alone knows what can turn our tears to laughter, our gloom to joy.

University of Georgia professor of psychology and leader of the atheist club at the school, Dr. Richard Suplita was often teaching atheism and arguing with Christians. Yet he still struggled with one aspect of atheism—the atheist worldview's existentialist crisis—the idea that if atheism is true, life is ultimately meaningless and not worth living. Suplita realized that the existential crisis extended far beyond the parameters of his own life. If atheism were true, it would mean the same things for the lives of his daughters, aged, ten, seven, and four. Suplita said that while he could spend time on the campus telling his students that there was no God, he could not bring himself to tell that to his own children. He just couldn't justify telling them that their lives were meaningless and that there was no God to glorify.

One day when a Christian speaker came to campus, he listened. Then he talked with some local church members who encouraged him to re-read the gospel of John and reconsider the truth of Christianity. A few weeks later, Suplita prayed to receive Christ as his Savior. He still believes the existential crisis is real, but he now understands its purpose is to point people to God. He says, "Only when you postulate an eternal God that you can actually have some sort of meaningful relationship with can you get around that existential crisis."

Only when he saw that there was life after death and a purpose for life here today did he have hope and a reason for getting up in the morning. Suplita said about his new faith, "It's helped give me peace in that sense, in that my life's about something and the lives of my daughters are about something that is lasting and enduring and can never fade away. And there is intrinsic hope in that."[3] The power of God brought to bear on hopelessness.

Hope is a by-product of the power of God, but as long as we think it is something we have to come up with ourselves, we won't ask Him for help with it, will we? Hope is just another of the many things God wants to provide for us that I always thought I had to provide. What a startling realization that has been to me!

Faithfulness to the End

There may be times in each of our lives when we're not sure we can continue on in our walk with Christ. We have grown so weary, so discouraged, so hopeless of any real change that we can't bring ourselves to try anymore. We were sure we'd always be faithful. We never imagined we'd ever feel so discouraged, such demoralizing pain of despair. It is in these moments that we most need to know that being faithful to the end is God's will for each of His children and that He promises to bring us the power to finish our race.

Our Lord wants each one of us to enter His kingdom and hear His "Well done my good and faithful servant, enter into the joy of your Master" (see Matthew 25:21). Since the ability to stay faithful when it is most difficult is among our many weaknesses, and yet faithfulness is His perfect will for us, we can be assured that it is something He will provide us the power to accomplish.

Therefore, since we have so great a cloud of witnesses surrounding us, let us also lay aside every encumbrance and the sin which so easily entangles us, and let us run with endurance the race that is set before us, fixing our eyes on Jesus, the author and perfecter of faith, who for the joy set before Him endured the cross, despising the shame, and has sat down at the right hand of the throne of God. For consider Him who has endured such hostility by sinners against Himself, so that you will not grow weary and lose heart (Hebrews 12:1–3).

Do you not know that those who run in a race all run, but only one receives the prize? Run in such a way that you may win. Everyone who competes in the games exercises self-control in all things. They then do it to receive a perishable wreath, but we an imperishable. Therefore I run in such a way, as not without aim; I box in such a way, as not beating the air; but I discipline my body and make it my slave, so that, after I have preached to others, I myself will not be disqualified (1 Corinthians 9:24–27).

It is Jesus who is the Author and Perfecter of our faith, not ourselves, or our parents, or our church, or our pastor, or our mentor. He's quite familiar with hostility, despair, and human weakness, for He experienced all of these things. It was His dependence upon His Father that saw Him through the worst of times. This is why He so often modeled this dependence and allows us to hear His prayers to His Father. We need to see how it is done.

Jesus didn't pull himself up by His boot straps; He called out in complete dependence upon His heavenly Father. Though He was fully God, He gave up the independent use of His divine attributes so that He might face the world on our terms and show us how to appropriate the power of His Father.

Here are only a fraction of things we can be sure are God's will for our lives, things for which He will surely be willing to provide His power. There are far, far more.

Strengthening His church
Obedience for godly living
Escape from temptation
Helping the weak and powerless
Sorrow over sin
Submission to authority
Living in His Spirit
Suffering for Him/sharing His sufferings

But though we want God's power in our lives, we often run into some daunting obstacles—from an unlikely source.

CHAPTER SIX

Overcoming Our Own Resistance to God's Power

The thing we have to watch most of all is our strength, our strong point. We all tend to fail ultimately at our strong point. —D. Martin Lloyd-Jones

Magnets are one of the more fascinating mysteries on earth. They are difficult to explain scientifically, but in layman's terms, natural and manufactured magnets have two ends, commonly called the north and south poles. When the north and south poles face each other, they attract magnetically. But when the north poles face each other, or the south poles face each other, they repel each other. If you've ever tried to push the same poles together, you've experienced this resistance yourself. You can't see it, but it's real.

We find something similar in the spiritual realm. Where we limit ourselves to our own human power, we will find His power repelled by the presence of our own. It is not that our power is equal to or greater than God's; it is that we have chosen our own power over His. He does not overrule our decision, but neither does He give us His power.

This might very well be the most difficult chapter in the entire book, because it calls for us to look at ourselves honestly and to recognize that *the greatest obstacle to the power of God in our lives is us!*

Obstacles to Choosing God's Power

Many may assume that because we want to see God's power manifested in our lives we would welcome it with open arms. Unfortunately, that's not true, because asking for God's power also involves abandoning confidence in our own, admitting failure, surrendering or releasing things we've held on to tightly—all things we are not comfortable doing.

Think of it this way: most of us at one time or another have needed to lose weight. We sincerely want to lose weight. The problem is that we also like eating. To lose weight involves curbing our appetite. In other words, something is acting against our desire to lose weight. Each time we think about losing weight we are faced with a choice that goes something like this:

Lose weight or eat that piece of pie.

Lose weight or eat that baked potato with butter, sour cream, cheese, and bacon.

Lose weight or have that sizzling, juicy steak.

Lose weight or eat some chocolate.

Lose weight or have that second, third, or fourth piece of pizza.

While the desire to lose weight is very real, and can even be intense, so is the obstacle to it. And the obstacle is not outside of us; it is inside. We do not fail because the truth is not available to us; we fail because we are resistant to the very truth we say we seek. Until we face the fact that there are personal reasons we choose something else over God's power in our lives, we will struggle to experience His power.

Now is the time for some serious introspection. If we are

going to appropriate the power God desires to make available to us, we have to look at the places in our lives where that power might be launched, and that means our weakness.

Our weakness.

This is not an easy sell, I know. How can I learn to be well content with the very things I'm most ashamed of and most afraid to look at?

There are two areas in our lives we need to examine: (1) those areas where we sense a clear and obvious weakness, and (2) those areas we've always seen as our strength. In these two contradictory areas we will find the same thing: places where God would demonstrate His power in our lives if we would only allow Him to.

It is natural to focus on our obvious weaknesses as areas where we need help, but in reality our areas of perceived strength might be where we gain the most illumination about our weaknesses. For example, Paul was a devout Jew, trained by the best teachers, admired and respected by his peers. But had it not been for the power of Christ in him, we would never have heard of the man. It was in his perceived strength that Paul needed to discover his weakness. He has not been a constant inspiration and known to millions because he was such a strong individual, but because the power of God was so clearly evident in his life. It's the same for us. We may have strengths in which we have tremendous confidence. History proves that we are gifted and competent in these areas. But sometimes that is where we are really experiencing the greatest weakness, because we have grown satisfied with displays of our human power and the accolades those draw to us, never imagining what the power of God applied to our strengths could look like.

It is the difference between a power generator and a bolt of lightning. The generator meets our expectations and needs, so we are satisfied with it, but it is paltry compared to the power of a bolt of lightning. Once Paul experienced God's power in His life he lost his appetite for what he could accomplish by his own efforts and talents.

We have difficulty receiving and experiencing the power of God in our lives because we already have something in its place. Our own power. Our confidence in our own power. Our excitement in our own power. Our comfort in our own power.

Does this mean I should seek to be weak? No, it means you already are—but haven't yet recognized it. So God will let you try out your strength, your plans, your programs, your methods, talents, energies, and abilities.

If we're honest, we will admit that we often experience little of significance in our activities—certainly nothing that corresponds to the blood, sweat, and tears we've put into the effort. We may pray fervently for success out of a genuine fear of failure, but frequently that's what our prayer really is: a prayer that we won't experience failure in our human efforts. This prayer will not release God's power on our behalf. God is not in the business of empowering our own efforts and plans so that we get the glory and His will is sidestepped. The two similar poles, God's glory and our own glory, our human power and God's power, will repel each other.

Seeking Backup Power

The demonstration of the power of God through the life of the average believer should be a given, not an anomaly. As Paul reminded a young pastor named Timothy, "God has not given us a spirit of timidity, but of power and love and discipline" (2 Timothy 1:7). However, as long as we believe we can do the job ourselves, we won't really seek His power in our lives. We will see anything God brings to bear on the situation as supplemental to seal our own efforts, an auxiliary reserve if you will—a sort of backup power source.

Many of us say prayers that *sound* right. We might pray, "Lord, we are totally dependent upon your power and intervention to accomplish this." We've been around long enough to know what kind of an attitude we should pose before God (and others). But that's often all it is—a pose—because what we are actually *placing our trust in* is not God working through our weaknesses to display His power, but our well-thought-out method, strategy, personal talent, drive, or aptitude to accomplish *what we've set out to do.*

If we believe we are failing because we just haven't learned how to do something the right way, or because we are using the wrong methods, or because our plan and approach just isn't good enough, or perhaps even because we aren't praying "the right prayer," then we will only be looking in some way to redouble our own efforts. We haven't yet come to the end of our own efforts. We are still in Madison Avenue mode: "We've just got to learn how to be better, smarter, faster."

Someone might readily say, "How can I really embrace my weaknesses when I have a fair amount of strengths? What if I'm smart, educated, and talented? Do I just pretend I'm weak? Wouldn't God see through that?" The answer is, yes, of course!

The issue isn't whether you have talents or abilities, but whether these, by themselves, will accomplish that which the power of God can accomplish through you. David was a courageous young man, but that alone would not have enabled him to beat Goliath; he wasn't counting on his own courage or his weapon to beat Goliath. What he had was a conviction that God would help him defeat this giant who, by defying and mocking

Israel, was defying and mocking his God. He was more than willing to stand up for God before Goliath—but only because he was convinced God would intervene to do something miraculous. If he was going to win this battle, it would be because God would empower a small shepherd with a primitive sling.

Recognizing Our Limitations

David was willing to take the abilities and strengths he had and show up—and from then on it was up to God. What was David expecting God to do in this titanic battle? Not much—just give him the perfect opening, the perfect rock, the perfect swing of his sling, the perfect aim to guide that rock to the only unprotected part of Goliath's head, and the perfect velocity to kill a giant of a man.

David's courage and natural talent couldn't guarantee that even half of these things would happen. Yet he believed God would intercede to help him in some way. Not in the sense that David believed he could probably take Goliath anyway, but it wouldn't hurt for him to throw up a prayer. David actually believed that his Lord could work powerfully through his weaknesses, disadvantages, and liabilities, and that when God did that, He would be glorified before His enemies as well as the Hebrews themselves.

Goliath had all the advantages of warfare, but David served the only living God. "And David said, 'The LORD who delivered me from the paw of the lion and from the paw of the bear, He will deliver me from the hand of this Philistine'" (1 Samuel 17:37).

David countered Goliath's weaponry with the name of his God! "Then David said to the Philistine, 'You come to me with a sword, a spear, and a javelin, but I come to you in the name of the LORD of hosts, the God of armies of Israel, whom you have taunted'" (17:45). David was seeking glory for God, not himself. "This day the LORD will deliver you up into my hands . . . that all the earth may know that there is a God in Israel" (17:46).

What we often miss, David didn't. *The Lord had delivered him in the past*, and it would have to be the Lord who delivered him against Goliath. His enemy came with all the latest military hardware and training; *David came in the name of the Lord of Hosts!* David knew that the Lord would defeat Goliath through him; it wouldn't be David's personal accomplishment. And David knew that the ultimate goal of this battle would be "that the earth may know that there is a God in Israel."

Part of stepping out in faith is the clear recognition of your own weakness and inability. Not the mouthing of those ideas as if that will obligate God, but in the heartfelt conviction that you are asking God to accomplish something you can't. This does not require a denigration of your talents and abilities or an insincere confession of weakness. You cannot bamboozle God. But even though you have strengths and talents, you need to recognize their limitations.

If we can't recognize the limitations of our own abilities and resources, we will never be able to embrace our weakness. We won't even really sense the need for God's power. We may theoretically agree we need God's power in our lives, but not practically.

Feeling Let Down

Many of us who have worked hard, prepared well, and applied the correct methodology to our vocations, marriage, parenting, and ministries have been disillusioned. We may have even met with what our world would term success. Yet the kind of impressive results we had hoped for have never materialized.

We wonder: Didn't I work hard enough? Do I lack drive and passion? Didn't I correctly or completely apply the methodology? Or do I just not have the skill set to see the results I truly longed for?

If we listen to the experts, the only reason we don't have a sizzling marriage is because we're simply not applying the right principles. If our children are having problems, it's because we're not parenting right and we need to follow the latest research by the latest Christian parenting expert. If our ministry is less than impressive, it's nothing that a seminar, or a conference, or a book or set of CDs by the latest spiritual guru won't fix.

Certain verses that seem to exhort us to follow the party line are thrown out again and again. But large segments of Scripture that seem to contradict this thinking are ignored. And what is ignored, over time becomes forgotten. Then one day we come upon the words of Paul, the apostle of weakness, who says he is well content with weakness, and while we would never disagree . . .

What are my own personal strengths? Preaching and encouraging. What are my weaknesses? Preaching and encouraging. I'm not trying to be clever here, just honest. At first I had to rely solely on God and His power to help me overcome my fear of being in front of people and my worry that I wouldn't know what to say or teach. But slowly, as God helped me, I gained more confidence and experienced what I came to call "success." Then I went to a Bible institute, and the knowledge I gained there made me feel far more comfortable teaching. Then I went to seminary where I learned how to preach "the right way." I was speaking at many different places and venues. I constantly received feedback that confirmed my abilities. My fear was gone. My sense of need was gone. Both had been replaced by my self-confidence.

I learned how to preach and encourage and lead well enough that I no longer felt a need for God's power. I still prayed for it, because, after all, I was a Bible student and I knew what I was supposed to pray for. Are you beginning to sense the problem?

When we are painfully aware of our weaknesses, we desperately seek God's power. When we become confident in our abilities, we cease asking for it, except in the most perfunctory way. We seek God's power the way we often give thanks at a meal, mindlessly and passionlessly. Our hearts and minds just aren't in it.

Paul, the apostle of power in weakness, was transparent before the churches he ministered with and to. As we look at his strengths and weaknesses, his areas of competence and incompetence, we will learn that both became potential sources of resistance to God's power. Let's begin with the areas that Paul considered his strengths and then move to his weaknesses.

Apostleship—His Personal Position

Paul reiterates to the Corinthian believers his Christ-given identity: "Am I not an apostle? Have I not seen Jesus our Lord? Are you not my work in the Lord?" (1 Corinthians 9:1). His apostleship was given to him by Jesus himself on the road to Damascus. The Corinthian believers were Christians in large part due to Paul's apostleship and ministry. If there was ever an appeal to power through personal position, Paul could make it.

Not too many things in this world trump the position of apostle of Jesus Christ, the Son of the Living God. Yet in this passage Paul is reminding the Corinthians that although he has the right to ask them for financial support, he isn't using that right. In fact, he reminds them that he refused to take any money from them, offering them his ministry in the gospel for free (9:18).

Many of us have personal power positions as well. Maybe you were born into wealth or status, or you have achieved those. Or perhaps you have a powerful personality, natural leadership ability, or some phenomenal talent.

As a pastor and author and parent I hold certain personal positions of power. The temptation is to assume that I don't really need God's power in these areas of my life—that I can handle them on my own. The tragedy is that our own positions of power are pathetically weak in comparison to what God's power could bring to bear on those positions.

The great apostle Paul recognized that human positions (even that of apostle) find their greatest fulfillment when God's power is applied to them. Have you ever sought to apply the power of God to your position(s) of power, or do you only ask Him for help where and when you feel weak?

Knowledge—His Personal Strength

The one area where Paul could unhesitatingly proclaim his strength was in the area of knowledge. "For I consider myself not in the least inferior to the most eminent apostles. But even if I am unskilled in speech, yet I am not so in knowledge; in fact, in every way we have made this evident to you in all things" (2 Corinthians 11:5–6). And it wasn't just Paul himself who claimed this. In a defense before a governor named Festus, in the presence of King Agrippa, the governor said, "While Paul was saying this in his defense, Festus said in a loud voice, 'Paul, you are out of your mind! Your great learning is driving you mad'" (Acts 26:24).

Knowledge, and his ability to use that knowledge in a variety of ways, was one of Paul's great strengths. Even his enemies admitted he was a highly intelligent and knowledgeable man.

Yet Paul's great strength could never bring him to a true knowledge of Jesus Christ. All the information he had at his disposal, all his vast intelligence could not help him perceive that Jesus was anything more than a charlatan.

It took Jesus appearing to Paul on the road to Damascus and revealing to him things he could not learn on his own to lead to his salvation. The most important truths Paul claimed were the result of special revelation—God revealing something to him he could not have learned otherwise, despite his brilliance. God took Paul's strength and empowered it to become so much more than it would have been otherwise.

All of us have personal strengths. Even those who are struggling with self-esteem will admit there is something we are good at. *These are the areas where we are least likely to seek the power of God in our lives.* God wants to take even your strengths and apply His power to them. Have you ever given Him the opportunity?

Pedigree—His Personal Advantage

When the Corinthians were in danger of being led astray by false prophets and apostles, Paul reminded them of his own credentials. "Are they Hebrews? So am I. Are they Israelites? So am I. Are they descendants of Abraham? So am I. Are they servants of Christ? . . . I more so" (2 Corinthians 11:22–23).

Since Paul's accusers were trumpeting their resumes, Paul sounded his own. He trumpeted his pedigree again to the Philippian church, as we will see in a moment, but at the end concluded: "But whatever things were gain to me, those things I have counted as loss for the sake of Christ. More than that I count all things to be loss in view of the surpassing value of knowing Christ Jesus my Lord, for whom I have suffered the loss of all things, and count them but rubbish so that I may gain Christ" (Philippians 3:7–8).

What are your personal advantages? Education, status, wealth, personality, confidence, physical strength, intelligence? All these things will help you in this life, but they won't help you experience the power of God in Christ Jesus. Yet these can be places where you can experience the power of God as you allow Him to display His power through your personal advantages.

Righteousness—His Personal Goodness

Paul reminded the Philippians, "If anyone else has a mind to put confidence in the flesh, I far more: circumcised the eighth day, of the nation of Israel, of the tribe of Benjamin, a Hebrew of Hebrews; as to the Law, a Pharisee; as to zeal, a persecutor of the church; as to the righteousness which is in the Law, found blameless" (Philippians 3:4–6). Paul was engaging in a little "no brag, just fact" here. When it came to religious goodness, he had the credentials.

It is tempting to put our confidence in what we have been able to achieve morally and religiously. Yet when we are convinced of our own goodness we are least likely to ask God to give us power to be holy, and it is the power of God alone that can lead to true godliness. When people on the outside looked at Paul's performance, everything looked great. But Paul knew God looked on the inside (Romans 7:15–25). He knew that his personal goodness, seen in external conduct alone, was skin deep and that his sin went to the bone. In this conflict, Paul proclaimed, "Wretched man that I am! Who will set me free from the body of this death? Thanks be to God through Jesus Christ our Lord!" (Romans 7:24–25). Whose power had set Paul free from the power of sin? God's!

So many Christians have convinced themselves that they have what it takes to live the Christian life without the power of God. They would never say it that way, but when they try to conquer their sinful habits, thoughts, and attitudes, they apply only their own street smarts, willpower, and clever Jedi mind tricks (remember the plastic pail over Old Faithful?). Our holiness is ornamental, decorative. We look holy, but inside we are just as sinful as we ever were, and we know it.

We believe that if we have a weakness of character or will, we should be able to overcome it. It's a matter of pride to us. And that's precisely the problem. The problem of sin runs far deeper than we think it does. The idea that we can overpower sin in our lives by ourselves is like a lone cowboy trying to lasso the space shuttle to keep it from taking off. This is also precisely why so many Christians do not live in moral or spiritual victory. They haven't yet realized that it's impossible apart from the power of God. What about you?

Special Revelation—His Personal Experiences

Paul is one of the few human beings who could say he had seen heaven while he still walked this earth. "I will go on to visions and revelations of the Lord. I know a man in Christ who fourteen years ago—whether in the body I do not know or out of the body I do not know, God knows—such a man was caught up to the third heaven. And I know how such a man—whether in the body or apart from the body I do not know, God knows—was caught up into Paradise, and heard inexpressible words, which a man is not permitted to speak" (2 Corinthians 12:1–4).

In a "last man standing" testimony contest, Paul would win. Every. Single. Time.

Amazing and unique experiences can be a source of great

pride and accomplishment. They can give us an authority and an audience that others don't have—and because of this make us feel special. Think of how many of our modern celebrities became famous because of an event that wasn't planned and yet catapulted them into national stardom (Joe the Plumber comes to mind).

Paul could have used his special revelation experience to bludgeon any who opposed him. How do you argue with a man who's been to Paradise and returned? I have seen a number of people use their personal experiences as a kind of authority for their words, ideas, and opinions—even when their experiences seemed to have little to do with the ideas and opinions they were now advertising. Paul didn't do that.

"On behalf of such a man will I boast; but on my own behalf I will not boast, except in regard to my weaknesses," he said. "For if I do wish to boast I will not be foolish, for I will be speaking the truth; but I refrain from this, so that no one will credit me with more than he sees in me or hears from me" (2 Corinthians 12:5–6). Paul realized he had been the recipient of a tremendous honor ("on behalf of such a man will I boast"), but he went on to confess that he refrained from talking a lot about it because it might cause people to "credit me with more than he sees in me or hears from me."

Have you been counting on your personal experiences to "empower" your Christian life or witness? While they certainly have a place and are important, it is not your experiences that can change hearts or deliver someone from sin or hell. It is only the power of the gospel of Christ; it is only Jesus. In fact, Paul went on to share that these very revelations required a "thorn in the flesh" to help keep him humble (12:7). I do not say this to belittle anyone's testimony, but only to warn that these experiences themselves are not the equivalent of the power of God.

Many amazing stories have powerful emotional punch, but when God adds His power to it, the punch turns into impact. We'll talk more about that later, but suffice it to say that even an amazing personal experience is not equivalent to the power of God.

Miracles—His Amazing Feats

When it comes to the miraculous, Paul's resume is superb. "The signs of a true apostle were performed among you with all perseverance, by signs and wonders and miracles" (2 Corinthians 12:12). Here was indisputable proof that God was blessing Paul's life—an amazing series of miraculous feats.

How easy it would have been for Paul to rest on his miracle-worker status for his authority in their lives. But he didn't do that. Instead of pointing at his miracles, he pointed to the power behind those miracles. As he said earlier, "On my own behalf I will not boast, except in regard to my weakness."

Supernatural power coursed through Paul in some way we can't understand. And although this happened numerous times, he chose not to call attention to it. What Paul wanted to highlight were his weaknesses. Why? Precisely because those very miracles were the greatest illumination of Paul's weaknesses. Whatever was accomplished through him supernaturally worked through the avenue of his weakness. There was simply no other option. Paul had no supernatural power of his own. None of us do.

Some of you may have accomplished amazing feats. You might be a war hero, a local hero, a brilliant musician, or a trend-setting businessperson. In some way you have accomplished what few have. If so, you may be sorely tempted to ride that horse all the way to the end of your race. Don't. It's a part of your life, an important part, and quite possibly something to be proud of (in a healthy manner). But amazing feats will not equal or come close to accomplishing what the power of God will in your life. Amazing feats are the business of yesterday, while the power of God is the stuff of today and tomorrow.

In his apostleship, his knowledge, his pedigree, his righteousness, his special revelation, and his miraculous feats, Paul was speaking of his strengths, his areas of competence or accomplishment. These were probably the areas where he was most tempted to bypass the power of God and go it alone. He chose not to, and that is instructive to us. But what about Paul's weaknesses; what about those areas where Paul reminds us that instead of being able to say "I'm competent," he is forced to say, "I'm helpless?"

It's quite a list.

Danger

Viciously flogged with thirty-nine lashes five times by the Jews, imprisoned, beaten so many times he couldn't remember, stoned, shipwrecked three times, in danger from swollen rivers and wild animals, betrayed by traitorous friends, endured sleepless nights, and exposed in the cold weather (2 Corinthians 11:23–27). Looking at this list of dangers Paul faced, we marvel that we escaped even half of them alive. In each and every case he was utterly helpless. Only the power of God could save him.

Are you in danger? Real danger? Utterly helpless? You are in a position to come before the God of all power and plead for His help.

Stress

"For even when we came into Macedonia our flesh had no rest, but we were afflicted on every side; conflicts without, fears within" (2 Corinthians 7:5). Conflicts without and fears within—sounds like stress to me. How did Paul overcome his stress? He didn't. He prayed and God answered: "But God, who comforts the depressed, comforted us by the coming of Titus" (2 Corinthians 7:6). Only God knew what would really comfort Paul, so He sent that comfort in the person of Titus, one of Paul's trusted traveling companions and friends.

Do you have conflicts without and fears within? If you are like me you do. Can the power of God touch us in the weakness of stress? The answer is yes!

Despair

We could even use the word *depressed* here. That certainly seems to be what Paul is describing in 2 Corinthians 1:8–9: "For we do not want you to be unaware, brethren, of our affliction which came to us in Asia, that we were burdened excessively, beyond our strength, so that we despaired even of life; indeed we had the sentence of death within ourselves so that we would not trust in ourselves, but in God who raises the dead." Paul and his companions were so depressed that they had given up hope of life itself.

Are you in that place right now? Are your problems so hard, so painful, so taxing that you "despair even of life," and you "have the sentence of death in yourselves"? Would it amaze you to learn that this is the exact place where God wants to demonstrate His power in your life?

You have already learned that you are in a situation you

can't fix, can't make better, and where you see no hope of anything good happening. Join Paul. Join the rest of us. We've all been there, and if we haven't, we will be.

What did God do for Paul in his weakness? He "delivered us from so great a peril of death, and will deliver us, He on whom we have set our hope. And He will deliver us" (2 Corinthians 1:10). The power of God delivered Paul when he could see no hope. That same power is available for you!

Inadequacy

Remember, Paul was "unskilled in speech" (2 Corinthians 11:6). He was the worst speaker and preacher among the apostles. In fact, Paul's inadequacies were legendary—everyone knew about them and talked about them—especially those who didn't like him and tried to use them against him.

We tend to avoid our areas of inadequacy, but Paul didn't avoid speaking and teaching. He used what ability he had over and over. But—and this is key—Paul sought God's power in his inadequacies. God never made Paul eloquent in public speaking; He made him something far more important—powerful! Do you remember the names of all those eloquent speakers in Paul's day? Neither does anyone else. Power in weakness!

Unimpressive

Paul's speech was "contemptible" and his personal presence was "unimpressive." (2 Corinthians 10:10). Paul was just not an impressive guy—in his day. The cold hard fact is that most of us fit into this category. In many ways we are simply unimpressive. We're not impressive physical specimens, we're not impressive intellectually, we're not impressive when it comes to our personality or accomplishments. This can be depressing . . . unless . . .

unless we realize that God would love to take our unimpressiveness and add His power to it to change our world. For His glory!

Baggage

I can already hear you. "Yeah, Dan, but you don't know about my baggage." I don't. But let's see if it compares with Paul's. "For I am the least of all apostles, and not fit to be called an apostle, because I persecuted the church of God" (1 Corinthians 15:9). Paul wasn't just being modest here; he was a real piece of work in his day. In Acts 8:1–3 we read that Paul assisted in murder and began "ravaging the church, entering house after house; and dragging off men and women, he would put them in prison." Sweet guy.

Bottom line: God doesn't care what your baggage is; His power can be demonstrated in spite of it and often even through it! Legal baggage, moral baggage, sexual baggage, religious baggage, relational baggage, none of it can dilute the power of God in your life—if you let God's power work through your weaknesses.

Fear

When Paul first began ministering in Corinth, he encountered danger and threats, and he was afraid. Paul, the great apostle, the guy who did miracles, was scared. Really, really scared. But God didn't scold Paul or tell him to get over it; He did something better. "And the Lord said to Paul in the night by a vision, 'Do not be afraid any longer, but go on speaking and do not be silent; for I am with you, and no man will attack you in order to harm you'" (Acts 18:9–10).

When fear hits us, it can be paralyzing. Are you really

afraid of something right now? Sometimes it seems like nothing can diminish our fear or make it go away, and we'd almost rather not live than live in constant fear. Paul knew the feeling and asked God to help him. God spoke to him at night, when our fears are often magnified the most. In quietness He promised His power to Paul to counter the very danger he so feared. That same God is still in business, and He's waiting to apply His power to your fear.

Abuse

Paul wrote honestly about the abuse he suffered: "in afflictions, in hardships, in distresses, in beatings, in imprisonments, in tumults, in labors, in sleeplessness, in hunger" (2 Corinthians 6:4–5). Some may find this language strange and foreign, but some of you will know exactly what Paul was talking about because you, too, have experienced or are experiencing abuse. You have been afflicted by others, bullied, physically abused, emotionally abused, or sexually abused. There is no one you can turn to. Until now.

Here, as well, God's power can be displayed. His heart is always with the weak, the afflicted, the destitute, and the humble. He waits for us to call upon Him.

Poverty

Contrary to what you might think if you watch many televangelists today, the early church apostles were poor. They didn't become rich on the gospel; in fact, they often lost everything. Paul himself knew what it was like to have plenty and to have very little. As he wrote to the Philippians, "Not that I speak from want, for I have learned to be content in whatever circumstances I am. I know how to get along with humble means, and I also know how to live in prosperity; in any and every circumstance I have learned the secret of being filled and going hungry, both of having abundance and suffering need" (4:11–12).

Paul knew hunger and need. He also knew that these were not punishments from God but opportunities to learn how to live in contentment and experience God's power regardless of whether he had a lot or a little. Have you learned that or is that one of your weaknesses? You may have learned the secret of being filled but not of going hungry.

Could we truly be content having less than what we do now? God's power can take us places our own power simply can't follow.

Sacrifice

Many people I know have been forced to do things they simply didn't want to do. They feel resentful, put out, wronged. They can't reconcile the idea of personal sacrifice being anything more than an evil. But Paul saw sacrifice as transforming. "For though I am free from all men, I have made myself a slave to all, so that I might win more" (1 Corinthians 9:19). Through Paul's willing self-sacrifice, God brought—and continues to bring through his inspired writings in Scripture—countless souls to salvation. This is called power through weakness.

I know people who have made themselves slaves to all in order to further the kingdom of God. They have given up their own conveniences, luxuries, and priorities to serve others, to put others' needs above their own. They are also the healthiest people I know. A quick glance around at our all-about-me culture will remind us this isn't the norm.

"For the kingdom of God does not consist in word but in

power" (1 Corinthians 4:20). When will we finally understand this? The resistance to God's power in our lives is found in the way we think about life, the way we think about ourselves, and the way we think about God. Our resistance is not just in our failure to admit our weaknesses; it is in our failure to see that our strengths are areas where we also need God's power.

But there is something else that can squelch our search for God's power. What about those times in our past when it seems God failed to help us?

Each of us has a history with God, and often that history is a stumbling block to further growth. What do we do when we have disappointments with how God worked in our lives in the past? Knowing God can help us isn't the same as believing that He will. It's time to look at an integral part of embracing our weakness—addressing past disappointments with God.

CHAPTER SEVEN

Understanding Past Disappointments

Have some of your carefully created castles been washed away? Mine have. Several times along my life's journey, I had nowhere to turn except into my heavenly Father's arms. There I remained quiet, soaking up His love for as long as I needed. Then I saw His hand begin a new creation in my life, a new direction, a new service for Him and His kingdom. Waves need not always destroy. We must allow our heavenly Father to use them to direct our lives. —JEAN OTTO[1]

The ability to cede to God our control and power often hinges on our willingness to allow God to be God. And this hinges on our belief or disbelief that God is precisely who and what He says He is. He not only calls himself our heavenly Father, but, since so many of us have had poor, absent, or twisted father images, He also reminds us through parable and example that He's a good Father who loves to give good gifts to His children, generously.

One of our struggles in this area is the problem of understanding the love of God as Father. Graciously, God has allowed me to be a human father and experience father love in a practical way in my own life. I need to start by saying that I have no words that truly and completely express the love I have for my three children. While *love, adore,* and *cherish* certainly apply, they still fall short. There are some things in life that the human language simply cannot do justice to, and a good parent's love for his or her children is one. Notice that I said "good" parent. The physical ability to produce offspring does not make one a good parent, as we are so frequently reminded in the news.

While I have the deepest love possible for my children, there were times when they must have felt that I did not really love them very much. Often their young hearts and minds yearned for something that would satisfy their own desires, but that Annette and I realized would not be good for them. My children would have loved nothing more than to eat sweets for breakfast, lunch, and dinner. They did not understand issues like nutrition, health, and moderation. So when they did not get all they wanted from us, they felt (rightly) that we were withholding something that would bring them instant pleasure. They saw only the fact that we would not give them what they wanted.

When my oldest daughter, Christi, was still a toddler, Annette and I took a long road trip. About an hour or two into the trip, Christi, sitting in a car seat between us in our old Toyota pickup, began to cry. She was clearly frustrated about something. We tried giving her milk, but as soon as she had finished it, she started crying again. We tried many different things to distract her from what was bothering her, but to no avail. When we stopped and let her out of the car, she was fine. When she got back in again, the frustrated crying began.

What made it worse was that she was sitting right between

us. She was accustomed to having us pick her up and comfort her when she was in distress, but since we were driving we couldn't do this without endangering her. I distinctly remember her little hands reaching out to grab my right hand and hold it tenderly. Then she'd get frustrated with me and push my hand away. Then, a few minutes later, she'd reach out for my hand again. Her actions continued the entire trip. In her young mind, we certainly had the power to help her, but we just weren't doing it.

Sound familiar?

The Unfortunate Conclusion

So many of our experiences with God are like this, especially when our requests seem eminently reasonable: money for rent, a new job, health for a loved one or yourself. We ask for something we are sure would be good for us and bring us pleasure and happiness, or we ask for the removal of something that is causing us pain or distress. We are not asking for anything sinful. When we do not receive what we ask for, we decide that God isn't really as good as we thought—at least not to us.

Or, we see others receiving precisely what we asked for and did not receive—like my children would see other parents buying their children the toy or candy or ice cream they were being denied at the moment. The conclusion we come to is that God just isn't that good—to us. We may never come out and say this, but the idea lingers in the shadows of all our thoughts of Him.

When he was in his late fifties, British author and scholar C. S. Lewis unexpectedly found love. He married an American woman named Joy Davidson, but almost immediately after their marriage, she was discovered to have cancer. They enjoyed only a few years of wedded bliss before the cancer took her life.

Lewis was broken and hurting. He later wrote a book called *A Grief Observed*, in which he told of the dangers his faith faced during this experience. "Not that I am (I think) in much danger of ceasing to believe in God. The real danger is of coming to believe such dreadful things about Him. The conclusion I dread is not 'So there's no God after all,' but 'So this is what God's really like. Deceive yourself no longer.'"[2]

In that same book he wrote, "Bridge players tell me that there must be some money on the game 'or else people won't take it seriously.' Apparently it's like that. Your bid—for God or no God, for a good God or the Cosmic Sadist, for eternal life or nonentity—will not be serious if nothing much is staked on it. And you will never discover how serious it was until the stakes are raised horribly high; until you find that you are playing not for counters or for sixpences but for every penny you have in the world."[3]

It is probably this idea that causes untold anxiety and stress in our lives. Unable to relax and trust that our God is a good heavenly Father who truly does want to give His children good gifts, we try to find ways to either (1) convince God of His oversight and neglect or (2) try to find ways to circumvent God altogether. It is here where praying for or asking for His power in our lives can so easily get sidetracked. It is difficult to get some Christians to even entertain ideas about God wanting to give them so much more than they can imagine, because in their past they haven't gotten some of the things they most wanted. So they have unwittingly learned to circumvent God altogether. They become like the child who thinks, "If Dad won't give me any candy or ice cream then I'll have to find another way to get what I want. After all, there's always Grandma!"

When we finally trust, truly trust the real character of our heavenly Father, then, and only then, will we be able to rest, with peace and contentment, in His will for us. Think about it. If you trusted God that He was indeed a good heavenly Father who loved you and delighted in giving you good things, would you stress over things you weren't getting, or even over things that He might take away?

How distorted is our image of God that we can only see Him as a good God if He gives us all the good things our hearts desire. How weak is our understanding of His wisdom and love and power that we cannot trust Him with the things we cherish most in life. When God gives us what we want, we praise Him, or, at the very least, have pleasant thoughts about Him. When He withholds that thing we most want—or worse, removes from us something we sought always to have or keep—we feel He is no longer good and thus not really to be trusted.

Paul could write these amazing words, "I am well content with weaknesses," precisely because he had come to fully and completely trust the character of his Savior and heavenly Father. God didn't love Paul any more when He gave him something or made life easier for him then when He removed something from him or caused life to be more challenging. Though these experiences of loss or distress *felt different*, they were not really different in nature.

Acts of Transformational Love

Both God's giving and God's taking away were acts of love designed to create in Paul what both he and his heavenly Father most wanted—his transformation into the image of Christ.

Did God the Father love Jesus His Son? That sounds like a silly and even heretical question, doesn't it? The smallest child in Sunday school knows the answer. But remember again what

God, the good Father, allowed His only and beloved Son to endure on this earth. Jesus endured much suffering while His Father did not intervene to stop it. In fact, His Father *sent* His Son to do this! Yet Hebrews tells us that it all had a good purpose. "Jesus, the author and perfecter of faith, *who for the joy set before Him* endured the cross, despising the shame, and has sat down at the right hand of the throne of God" (Hebrews 12:2). Jesus knew His Father's goodness and was able to accept both plenty and want, joy and pain, success and failure as part of His good Father's will for Him. Both the pain and the loss had a final great purpose—joy!

When I don't see God as a good Father, losing anything is a clear negative; there is nothing good about it, and I must seek to manipulate circumstances with all my energy to forestall it. When I release my will to my good heavenly Father, I no longer have to do that.

When I finally rest in the truth that my heavenly Father is both absolutely sovereign in my life and completely and totally a good Father, I can gladly accept not only gain, but loss. If God is truly good and removes something or someone from my life, painful though it may be, there is a good reason for it. I must not try to understand what that reason is, for all my human intelligence will never comprehend the infinite wisdom of God. As He has said:

> "For My thoughts are not your thoughts,
> Nor are your ways My ways," declares the LORD.
> "For as the heavens are higher than the earth,
> So are My ways higher than your ways
> And My thoughts than your thoughts" (Isaiah 55:8–9).

Trust in the LORD with all your heart
And do not lean on your own understanding.
 In all your ways acknowledge Him,
And He will make your paths straight (Proverbs 3:5–6).

I have seen people who were very well off financially, or socially, or physically lose those resources. Yet, to a person, these people gained a maturity and Christlikeness that was missing from their lives before. They learned to trust their heavenly Father more because they had to, and trusting Him more led them to love Him more deeply as He met them in their time of deepest need. They hadn't been bad. This wasn't punishment. It was character development, and that's not always fun.

My goal in fathering wasn't simply to teach my children to obey; it was to assure them that I loved them deeply and that I was committed to doing whatever would be for their true good, whether that was taking them out of school for lunch at Taco Bell with Dad, or sending them to their room alone so they could begin to learn how to obey and become a more compassionate, responsible, Jesus-loving person one day. My love for them needed both to give and take away, to play with them eagerly as well as send them to their rooms for a time out; it involved hugs, kisses, and discipline when needed.

Revisiting Painful Places

We can embrace our weakness and trust God to reveal His power in the most difficult of our situations only, and most fully, when we have made peace with His goodness. Sometimes that involves willingness to finally revisit and reassess some of those experiences in our past where we have believed God did not truly act in our best interest, when we experienced pain, loss, discouragement, and allowed our heart to cast doubt on His goodness.

Ironically, sometimes to move forward in our relationship with Christ we must go backward to those places we feel He failed us. You may not think that's important, but I'll guess that if you've been a Christian for any length of time, you'll admit to a situation or event, or several situations or events, in your life where God did not act the way you thought He should.

You needed something desperately, and He didn't provide it. You wanted something passionately and it was denied you.

Something important was taken from you:

a person	an opportunity
a relationship	a house
your health	a dream or ambition
your reputation	a job
status or income	an ability or talent

Today, many have developed or bought into a strange hybrid Christianity that emphasizes only the positive and the feel-good: You'll have joy, peace, more money, a better marriage, better kids, and a more enjoyable life all around if you "join up." There has been confusion about the abundant life that Jesus promised us in John 10:10: "The thief comes only to steal and kill and destroy; I came that they may have life, and have it abundantly." That "abundance" is understood by this hybrid Christianity to be material abundance, success in all your endeavors, a constant happiness, and a brand-new and improved mental attitude.

While God can and often does visit His children with some

of these things, they should not be confused with the abundant life in Christ.

Understanding Truly Abundant Life

Abundant life in Christ is finally understanding what life is really all about—glorifying God—and entering into that blessed state where glorifying Him becomes the great overriding purpose of our existence. All of the other things we chase can bring temporary happiness, but it's a happiness that fades with time. Jesus' abundant life produces a stream of joy coming from our heavenly Father into our hearts. Now we are finally living life as it is meant to be lived, and we find our relationship with Him to be more satisfying than any other human pursuit or longing. As a result we do not require only positive things to happen in our life for us to experience true joy. We realize that transformation into the image of Christ will take not only addition to our lives, but also, at times, subtraction; not only gain, but pain; not only plenty, but scarcity.

Let's revisit a passage we looked at earlier and be reminded of what Paul's life of faith consisted of (2 Corinthians 11:23–30):

Labors

Imprisonments (more than one!)

Beatings (so many he forgot the exact number)

Constant mortal peril (the constant danger of death)

Beaten with rods three times

Stoned

Shipwrecked (three times!) — Paul spent one day and night in the ocean, probably clinging to pieces of the shipwreck before being rescued

Dangerous travels:

Danger from flooding and rivers

Dangers from robbers
Dangers from hostile Jews
Dangers in hostile cities
Dangers in the wilderness he frequently had to pass
through
Dangers on the sea voyages
Dangers among false friends.
Hard work, sleepless nights
Hunger
Thirst
In danger of cold and exposure on his frequent travels

Paul endured all those things, and yet his troubles and dangers would have stopped immediately had he recanted his faith in Christ. But he wouldn't do it. Why? Because he had found something immeasurably better than anything he was losing or enduring. Paul's relationship with Jesus was so precious and dear to him that whatever he had to endure to keep it was more than worth it.

Is that the nature of your faith? I am quite sure Paul would not recognize the type of Christianity often being advertised in churches today. Would he recognize ours?

Admittedly, Paul was an apostle, and he recognized the special sacrifice required of his calling:

For, I think, God has exhibited us apostles last of all, as men condemned to death; because we have become a spectacle to the world, both to angels and to men. We are fools for Christ's sake, but you are prudent in Christ; we are weak, but you are strong; you are distinguished, but we are without honor. To this present hour we are both hungry and thirsty, and are poorly clothed, and are roughly treated, and are homeless; and we toil, working with our own hands; when we are reviled, we bless; when we are persecuted, we endure; when we are slandered, we try to conciliate; we have become as the scum of the world, the dregs of all things, even until now (1 Corinthians 4:9–13).

Even though this is true, however, how can we account for his passion, his joy, his willingness to die for the very faith Jesus led him into? He never expresses any regret at abandoning his comfortable and prestigious and respected life to follow Jesus; in fact, just the opposite.

But whatever things were gain to me, those things I have counted as loss for the sake of Christ. More than that, I count all things to be loss in view of the surpassing value of knowing Christ Jesus my Lord, for whom I have suffered the loss of all things, and count them but rubbish so that I may gain Christ, and may be found in Him, not having a righteousness of my own derived from the Law, but that which is through faith in Christ, the righteousness which comes from God on the basis of faith, that I may know Him and the power of His resurrection and the fellowship of His sufferings, being conformed to His death; in order that I may attain to the resurrection from the dead (Philippians 3:7–11).

If we don't understand the true purpose of the Christian life, which is to glorify God, we will frequently be at odds with God about any uncomfortable experiences He is allowing in our lives, as well as what He's removing from our lives. When our lives don't look like the ones being advertised in some Christian circles, we can feel we've been cheated.

The Danger of Externalized Christianity

But such Christianity is an externalized Christianity. It's all about what's happening *to* me, good or bad, not what God's starting to do *in* me! Real Christianity transforms us slowly into the image of Jesus, and that involves a considerable amount of tweaking in literally every area of our lives.

If pride is present (which it always is), humbling will be necessary. We like our pride—we have very little intention of letting it go voluntarily. At times God will remove the object of our pride because it is keeping us from humility before Him. This is not punishment; it is transformation. Pride forces our attention on ourselves—and there is no joy in that. Humility focuses our attention on Christ, and there we find great joy. The end goal of the process is not deprivation but replacement of an empty, futile, self-preoccupation with a heart that can finally see the glory of God and revel in His presence and love.

We could go on and on about what God might, at times, need to remove from our lives, or replace in our lives, or add to our lives to bring about a heart and mind that rejoices in the only pure and worthwhile thing in the entire world—God! For a tree to bear good fruit, it requires not only things given to it (water, fertilizer, good soil, sun) but also branches cut from it. A carefully pruned tree bears far more fruit than one that has been ignored.

A Christianity that recognizes no need of pruning in our lives is an ornamental Christianity. It's like a beautiful Christmas tree we cut down at the Christmas tree farm. We bring it home, stick it in water, and decorate it. It's charming and beautiful. It's also lifeless. All the decorations and lights in the world won't be able to stop the tree from eventually turning brown, brittle, ugly, and dangerous. It's bound to happen—because we were decorating a dead tree.

So much modern Christianity seems to be about decorating a dead tree as we seek to hang onto the very things that need to die—like greed, anger, jealousy, bitterness, gossip, pride, and lust. God wants to provide us the power to be transformed from death into life, from chasing the very things that bring heartache and ruin to pursuing the only things that bring true joy and fulfillment.

When we try to deduce the character of God from our history with Him, we need to view it through the lens of His goal of transforming us into the image of Christ. He will add and He will prune in order to form us into the image of His Son. When we resist this transformation process, seeing only inconvenience, pain, or loss, we forget or deny the very purpose of our existence—to glorify God. We glorify Him when we become more like Him, desiring what He desires, loving what and how He loves.

We Need Pruning

Whether we want to admit it or not—and often we don't—if we are to become more like Jesus, we need to be pruned of things we won't let go of voluntarily.

Sometimes we value relationships with others over Him
Sometimes we value our pride and confidence over Him
Sometimes we value our status over Him
Sometimes we value our knowledge or intelligence over Him
Sometimes we value our position over Him.

God may need to remove (cut) or alter things in our lives

(prune). If that has happened to you in the past and you assumed God wasn't being very good or loving toward you, you need to revisit that event. Even if you still don't know why God allowed it, you can admit that He always has a purpose in your life and that He proved forever His character and love toward you on the cross.

Our Lord suffered horribly in much of His earthly life. Furthermore, none of what He had to endure was deserved. There was no sin in His life causing it, no need for transformation in His character or nature. In fact, all of our Lord's suffering was the result of someone else's sin. My sin. Your sin.

Jesus called His Father a good Father! Yet God the good Father allowed His Son:

To be poor

To be misunderstood

To be slandered

To be in constant danger

To suffer abandonment

To be isolated in His time of greatest suffering

To be rejected and crucified by the very people He had come to save

The Scriptures unapologetically remind us that whom God loves He prunes to be more like His Son, Jesus. Hebrews 12 reminds us of that and encourages us not to grow weary and lose heart.

> For consider Him who has endured such hostility by sinners against Himself, so that you will not grow weary and lose heart. You have not yet resisted to the point of shedding blood in your striving against sin; and you have forgotten the exhortation which is

addressed to you as sons, "MY SON, DO NOT REGARD LIGHTLY THE DISCIPLINE OF THE LORD, NOR FAINT WHEN YOU ARE REPROVED BY HIM; FOR THOSE WHOM THE LORD LOVES HE DISCIPLINES, AND HE SCOURGES EVERY SON WHOM HE RECEIVES." It is for discipline that you endure; God deals with you as with sons; for what son is there whom his father does not discipline? But if you are without discipline, of which all have become partakers, then you are illegitimate children and not sons. Furthermore, we had earthly fathers to discipline us, and we respected them; shall we not much rather be subject to the Father of spirits, and live? For they disciplined us for a short time as seemed best to them, but He disciplines us for our good, so that we may share His holiness. All discipline for the moment seems not to be joyful, but sorrowful; yet to those who have been trained by it, afterwards it yields the peaceful fruit of righteousness (Hebrews 12:3–11).

"Afterwards it yields the peaceful fruit of righteousness."
Peaceful fruit of righteousness. Abundant life.
Afterward.
After the discipline. After the adding. After the cutting. After the pruning.
Afterward.

We Need to Reconsider

James the apostle writes, "Consider it all joy, my brethren, when you encounter various trials, knowing that life can be a real bummer and totally unfair!" (Sorry, that's not what he actually said).

131

What James actually writes is, "Consider it all joy, my brethren, when you encounter various trials, knowing that the testing of your faith produces endurance. And let endurance have its perfect result, that you may be perfect and complete, lacking in nothing" (James 1:2–4).

James says that the end result of the trials that come our way will, if we allow them, make us perfect and complete. Now, who do you know who is perfect and complete? Wait . . . that would be Jesus! God's purpose in our lives is not to make us miserable; it is to make us into the image of Jesus, who alone is perfect and complete, lacking in nothing. There is wisdom to be gained through the difficulties God brings our way—wisdom that comes no . . . other . . . way.

Later in the same book, James encourages Christians to be wise and understanding.

> Who among you is wise and understanding? Let him show by his good behavior his deeds in the gentleness of wisdom. But if you have bitter jealousy and selfish ambition in your heart, do not be arrogant and so lie against the truth. This wisdom is not that which comes down from above, but is earthly, natural, demonic. For where jealousy and selfish ambition exist, there is disorder and every evil thing. But the wisdom from above is first pure, then peaceable, gentle, reasonable, full of mercy and good fruits, unwavering, without hypocrisy. And the seed whose fruit is righteousness is sown in peace by those who make peace (James 3:13–18).

James contrasts some of the things he knew were in the hearts of his flock (jealousy, selfish ambition, disorder, and every evil thing) with what God wanted to put into the hearts of those same people: abundant life; the peaceful fruit of righteousness; the wisdom from above.

Are you beginning to sense a pattern in the New Testament? This is where God intends to bring us—this is His goal. It is a wonderful life, full of peace, righteousness, wisdom, joy, and fulfillment. But it's not often where we're at today, is it?

What's hard is that for us to get that very life we want, a part of our life has to be pruned, a part needs to be cut, we need to experience loss and the removal of attitudes and things that we might cherish (at the moment) more than the transformation God wants to do in us. We will rarely see, especially at the moment, the connection between what is painful and what He is doing in us. All discipline, as the writer of Hebrews says, is not joyful.

Christian philosopher Peter Kreeft of Boston University was once trying to explain why God might tolerate certain short-range evils to achieve long-range goods that humans cannot foresee. He asks us to imagine a bear in a trap and a hunter who wants to liberate him. The hunter tries and fails to win the bear's confidence, so he has no choice but to shoot the bear full of tranquilizers. The terrified bear thinks the hunter is trying to kill him. He doesn't understand that the hunter is acting out of compassion to save him.

There are moments when God's actions don't seem good. But they are. He is a *good* Father. Wanting to make you more like Jesus is an act of amazing love on His part. And being more like Jesus will bring you greater joy than any other thing in life.

A cancer specialist listens to a person's description of his or her symptoms and then orders the proper tests to determine if there is cancer in the body. If the tests come back positive, the doctor orders the appropriate treatment plans, seeking to remove the cancer. The patient must trust the doctor, even when much of what the doctor advises may be painful or uncomfortable, or both. Often surgery is required to remove a cancer— to "prune" away that which might destroy the patient.

We put up with all of this, even though we rarely understand all of the issues involved in the treatment of cancer, because we know two things: (1) cancer can kill us, and (2) the doctor is trying to help us.

In the same way, you will not always understand why God has allowed you to suffer, to experience unexplainable loss, to be mistreated. But you can understand that you have a spiritual cancer known as sin and that God's surgery to cut it out of you will be to make you more like Jesus who knew no sin.

The absence of sin doesn't create an empty void in us; instead, it fills us with peace, joy, and contentment. God's purpose is not just removal, but *replacement*. So many people think God's real purpose in our lives is to get us to stop sinning. What they don't understand is that sin is the obstacle to the real joy we long for. The healthy Christian is not a passionless creature who has been neutered of sin through a spiritual lobotomy, but someone who has finally begun to experience what life is really all about and is living for the first time in the joy that produces. The *abundant* life.

To ask God to help us in our weakest, most vulnerable moments is an act of trust, and we aren't likely to do this if we don't believe He is trustworthy. If you thought the surgeon who was scheduled to cut the cancer out of your body wasn't trustworthy, would you let him or her put you to sleep and begin carving you up?

Some people have that attitude toward God. While they

feel He is totally qualified to empower their weaknesses, something in their past makes them hesitate to believe that He will. It may be several large things or one rather small thing, but it casts at least a shadow of a doubt on God's goodness to them.

It's time to recognize that God is completely and totally good by nature and cannot do anything that is not in keeping with His perfect righteousness. His goodness springs from His eternal love toward us.

We Need to Trust

I encourage you to revisit those events and experiences that have caused you to question God's goodness. Even if they happened years ago, look at them through a new lens—the lens of God's purpose of transforming you into the image of Jesus. Recognize that even if you still can't understand why He allowed it, His purpose has always been to transform you into the image of Christ.

To give you more abundant life.

To enable you to experience the peaceful fruit of righteousness.

In 2011 Steve Jobs, the famous co-founder of Apple, died of pancreatic cancer. When his pancreatic neuroendocrine tumor was discovered in October of 2003, doctors told him he was lucky that they had caught it so early and that it could be removed before spreading—which it would definitely do if left untreated. But, in his own words, "I really didn't want them to open up my body, so I tried to see if a few other things would work." These "other things" included a strict vegan diet, acupuncture, herbal remedies, and other alternative techniques—even consulting a psychic.

Though his family begged him to get the surgery, he

refused—until a 2004 CAT scan revealed that the tumor had grown and perhaps spread. He discovered that he could not make the cancer go away under his own power. He had surgery to remove part of his pancreas, but by then the cancer had spread to three spots on his liver.[4]

Though his doctors continued to give Jobs advice about the good nutrition his body needed and some additional procedures that could help, he ignored or resisted much of it, until finally it was just too late. The doctors might have saved his life had he fully entrusted himself to them. But he didn't. The power to save his life was available. The problem wasn't knowledge, it was trust.

And so we come back to you and me and the empowered, abundant life. And it all comes down to trust, doesn't it? Do you *trust* God to empower your life? His power is available and waiting, but it must be requested.

The One who wields power for you is a good Father. Let that sink in. Deeply. Whenever you doubt it, return to the cross.

Take a quiet moment here, in prayer, and revisit a place or places where God allowed something in your life that was or is painful and confusing. As you look at that event, look beyond it to your God hanging on the cross for you, dying for you. Begin to see God's activity in your life as He sees it, an act of transformational love, designed not to destroy or punish you but to slowly and deliberately transform you more into the image of Jesus.

Confess to God your confusion—your honest confusion—but also your trust in His character, no matter how weak that trust might be at this moment. Ask God to show His power in your weakness here, where it is hard, to help you trust Him again.

Okay. Now, how does all this work?

CHAPTER EIGHT

The Rest-Release Program

The weaker we feel, the harder we lean on God. And the harder we lean, the stronger we grow.
—JONI EARECKSON TADA

A year or so ago when Annette and I were in a local Costco we stopped by the Verizon kiosk. She needed a new phone, and although she didn't see anything she wanted, she pointed out one she thought I might like. The salesman eagerly began showing me all the things this amazing little Droid X could do. It could talk to you with its GPS, it could text in several different cutting-edge ways, it could surf the Internet at high speed, it could jump tall buildings in a single bound! It was pretty neat. I was so impressed that I bought it. One problem: the guy who sold me the phone knew how to do all those wonderful things with it. I didn't! It took me forever to learn how to use all those functions the salesmen showed me.

There are few things more frustrating than being offered a wonderful new experience but not being able to fully take advantage of it because, frankly, you don't know how it works. And that's what we're going to address in this chapter. We need to start asking, in a very practical way, how does this "embracing our weakness" actually work in real life? And I think one of the best ways to do this is to show in Scripture how several folks used this embracing-our-weakness strategy before the apostle Paul ever showed up on the scene.

It has *always* been God's will that His people learn to embrace their weakness so they can witness His power in their lives. So I'd like to take us to two Old Testament kings of Israel, King Asa and King Jehoshaphat. The situations in which they needed God's power were dire and urgent. They needed His power or they were sunk.

Historical Testimonies

Let's start with King Asa in 2 Chronicles 14:1–11, and we'll begin with this brief biography of him: "Asa did good and right in the sight of the LORD His God, for he removed the foreign altars and high places, tore down the sacred pillars, cut down the Asherim, and commanded Judah to seek the LORD God of their fathers and to observe the law and the commandment. He also removed the high places and the incense altars from all the cities of Judah. And the kingdom was undisturbed under him" (vv. 2–5).

I love these biographies in the Old Testament where an entire life of decisions and experiences and activities is summed up in one paragraph, or even in one phrase: "Asa did good and right in the sight of the LORD." This is important, and we'll speak more about why later.

We find out in this chapter that Zerah the Ethiopian attacked Israel with a 1,000,000-man army plus 300 chariots, which were the tanks of those days. King Asa had about 600,000 troops and no tanks. It was 2 to 1 in favor of the Ethiopians. One of the main goals in military warfare is to have numerical superiority. Asa and Israel knew how to count, and they knew they were in serious trouble.

Asa's Confession: "Then Asa called to the LORD, his God, and said, 'LORD, there is no one besides You to help in the battle between the powerful and those who have no strength; so help us, O LORD our God, for we trust in You, and in Your name have come against this multitude. O LORD, You are our God; let not man prevail against You'" (v. 11).

Do you hear any bravado or ego in these words? The *powerful* were the Ethiopians; the ones with *no strength* were the Hebrews. Asa's first reaction, his confession, consisted of a number of truth statements:

God, you're the only one who can save us (we know how this *should* turn out).

Our enemies are powerful. We, on the other hand, have no strength (we can't fix this).

But we trust in you and in your name (we think you can fix this).

We have, therefore, come forth in your name (we're *trusting* you to fix this).

Please, don't let these folks prevail against you (not us, you).

And then they fought a battle!

Asa's Results: "So the LORD routed the Ethiopians before Asa and before Judah, and the Ethiopians fled . . . they could not recover . . . they were shattered" (vv. 12–13). God's power displayed in their weakness.

They fought a battle against all odds, the Lord routed the Ethiopians before them, and they were victorious in follow-up battles as well, receiving much plunder in the process from those who planned to kill and plunder them.

Now let's move on a few chapters to King Jehoshaphat. In

2 Chronicles 17:3–4 we read his biography: "The LORD was with Jehoshaphat because he followed the example of his father David's earlier days and did not seek the Baals, but sought the God of his father, followed His commandments, and did not act as Israel did." King Jehoshaphat wasn't posturing for the public; his faith was the real deal.

But in 2 Chronicles 20 we read that the sons of Moab, the sons of Ammon, and the Meunites came to make war against Jehoshaphat. They are described as "a great multitude." Again, as with Asa, we find no bravado in Jehoshaphat. We hear no "Bring it on!" statements. In fact, Jehoshaphat "was afraid and turned his attention to seek the LORD" (v. 3).

Jehoshaphat's Confession: "O our God, will You not judge them? *For we are powerless before this great multitude* who are coming against us; nor do we know what to do, but our eyes are on You" (v. 12).

Let's make sure we clearly see what Jehoshaphat is saying here:

We are powerless before them (we can't fix this, we don't know what to do).

But our eyes are on you, Lord (we know you aren't powerless before them).

Then we see God's response to Jehoshaphat's confession: "'Do not fear or be dismayed because of this great multitude, for the battle is not yours but God's . . . . You need not fight in this battle; station yourselves, stand and see the salvation of the LORD on your behalf, O Judah and Jerusalem.' Do not fear or be dismayed; tomorrow go out to face them, for the LORD is with you" (vv. 15, 17).

Jehoshaphat's Results: How did God demonstrate His power in their weakness? "When they [the Hebrews] began singing and praising, the LORD set ambushes against the sons of

Ammon, Moab and Mount Seir, who had come against Judah; so they were routed. For the sons of Ammon and Moab rose up against the inhabitants of Mount Seir destroying them completely, and when they had finished with the inhabitants of Seir, they helped to destroy one another" (vv. 22–23).

In both these situations God's power was displayed in their weakness. Sound familiar? In both these situations we see obedience to what God had called them to do in spite of their weakness and fear, and then faith that He would do what they couldn't in spite of their strength and weaknesses.

Now, before we begin to see what we are to do in our situations, I want to point something out. When a problem, or a challenge, or a calamity arises in your life, *you already react a certain way*. You've developed habits you don't even realize you have. We need to visit that for a moment. Because before we can do something different, we need to:

Change Our First Reactions

What are your first reactions? For many they are *negative*:

I quit!	I'm going to fail!
This will destroy me.	I'll never survive this.
This is just impossible.	I can't beat this.
I'm not up to this.	I can't bring myself to do this.

Others are *positive*.

I can handle this.	This is just a speed bump.
This won't beat me.	I'm *not* going to fail!
I'll figure this out.	I'm strong!
I believe in myself.	I will survive!

141

Each of us has a normal default in most situations. Some of us are positive, we-can-beat-this kind of people; others of us are negative, I'll-never-beat-this kind of people. Neither response is correct.

You see, either way, *we are focusing on ourselves*, not on God and what He might want to do in the situation. And both reactions are difficult to overcome. When you've learned to quit, to surrender, to imagine failure in all you do, *your eyes are constantly on your weakness*, not His power. When you've learned to think positively, to believe in yourself and your own ability to succeed, *your eyes are constantly on your own power*, not on His. In both reactions we are finding the answer to the test or challenge within ourselves—ignoring God and His power that is available to us.

Embracing our weakness involves taking our eyes off our own skills, talents, and resources as well as our own liabilities, weaknesses, and past failures. None of those things has anything to do with the power of God in us, whether we feel strong and gifted or weak and helpless. Neither extreme is the proper position before God.

In our weakest moments God can deliver us in a mighty way, and in our strongest moments He can do far beyond what our human strength and giftedness can accomplish. However we might feel, or whatever pose we might strike, we are weak and powerless before almighty God.

In Psalm 8:3–4 we read, "When I consider Your heavens, the work of Your fingers, the moon and the stars, which You have ordained; what is man that You take thought of him, and the son of man that You care for him?" In Psalm 103:14 we read, "For He Himself knows our frame; He is mindful that we are but dust."

Whatever our first reaction is to weakness or challenges, if it isn't seeking His power first and foremost, we need to change.

Exchange Power Paradigms

This is where we begin to learn *how* to request God's power, and there is nothing complicated or mysterious here. There is no secret insider information we need to know. We just first need to admit, as we saw above, that we *don't* seek His power first, or even often, in the situations we encounter.

Now let's look at five steps to requesting God's power in your life.

Step One: *Don't bother unless you are sincere.* There is no magic prayer or approach that obligates God to do anything He doesn't want to do. But, as we've already seen, God *desires* to display His power in our lives for His glory. Unless your desire is to truly obey and glorify God, to seek His power for your own purposes is an exercise in futility. God cannot be bamboozled into doing our bidding by some secret approach or special prayer. Remember the bios of King Asa and King Jehoshaphat? They *walked* with God; they sought to *glorify Him* in their lives. They *humbled themselves* before God and were willing to receive His answer.

But notice I said your *desire* must be to glorify God. You may not feel like you are always successful at obeying and glorifying Him, but that's completely understandable—you're not. Remember, Jesus asked His closest disciples in the garden of Gethsemane to stay awake and watch with Him, and yet they fell asleep. He said, "The spirit is willing but the flesh is weak" (Matthew 26:41). It is not perfection that launches His power, but a desire in our hearts to glorify Him in what we are asking, even in the midst of our imperfections. *We were made to glorify Him; that is what He is eager to do in us, in ways we cannot begin to imagine.*

How do you know whether or not your request will glorify Him? You'll know you are seeking to glorify Him when you are willing to receive *whatever* He gives you.

When I was about twenty-two years old, I began to ask God to relieve me of a stomach issue that was distressing to me, and He did. . . twenty-eight years later!

Doctor after doctor told me I had colitis, or irritable bowel syndrome, even though none of those symptoms really fit my situation. At a certain point I accepted that this was God's will for my life for His purposes, and I often asked for His power to endure suffering. Everyone suffers from something; I just figured that this ailment was my something. When people talked about physical suffering, I truly empathized and prayed for them, in a way I never would have before. When someone talked about an illness that just wouldn't go away, I understood. I thought I'd have mine until I died.

I learned many things in my suffering, things nothing else could have taught me. Then, it glorified God to remove my suffering, and He did that as well. I discovered that my gall bladder was bad and needed to be removed. I had that done and my suffering vanished.

One day I will suffer again from something, and ultimately die of it. And then my suffering will be over forever. God's power will transform me from death and suffering into eternal glorious life with Him forever.

Step Two: *Confess your need or weakness.* There is some issue, some obstacle, some fear, some challenge for which you need His power. Be honest and simply tell God that you can't fix this situation. You need His power; you are unable or feel unable to do what it is you need to do. This is accepting your helplessness—something difficult for us to admit.

You can't bypass this step. You aren't telling God anything He doesn't know, but you are the one who needs to hear it again.

Step Three: *Request His power in your life.* "Lord, may you demonstrate your power in my life in this area. Where I am weak, may you demonstrate your power in my weakness. I desire to see your power in my life, not my own. Lord, show me your power that I may glorify you and that you may be glorified."

Step Four: *Do what He has called you to do in this situation.* God does often call us to do something. Seeking His power does not involve sitting idly by. Remember King Asa and the children of Israel were called to actually go to battle against great odds. They had to fight, but God promised them, *promised them,* that He would give them the victory. With King Jehoshaphat we saw that God did not ask him and his army to fight, but to show up, station themselves before Him, and honor Him with singing and praise. Yet in a battle situation, even showing up and making yourself visible to the enemy is a step of faith.

If we need God's power to do something in our lives, we don't just sit back and wait for some divine power dump. God often wants us to act, and then He supernaturally empowers our actions or the responses we will receive.

If God has called us to forgive someone and we feel we can't, we can ask for His power in this and He will give it— but we still have to intend to forgive. If we are asking God to help us physically, that doesn't mean we don't keep our doctor's appointment, but that we are trusting God to work through, and even beyond, our doctor.

I went to five doctors over the course of twenty-eight years seeking relief from my stomach issue. None of them diagnosed me properly. Finally, I went online and began doing research on gall bladder disease and realized that most often doctors are looking for gall stones to indicate a problem. But I never had gall stones. My gall bladder just wasn't working properly and no one realized that. I found that one particular gall bladder disease matched my symptoms perfectly. Perfectly! Then I went to the doctor and asked to have my gall bladder removed. He ran some tests and discovered that, yes, my gall bladder was not functioning properly. In fact, it needed to be removed immediately if not sooner. It was removed and my pain and suffering were gone.

If you have a daunting obstacle to overcome, a confrontation, a situation where you need to do something, you may still need to do it, but realize that your effort won't be enough and that you are asking for God to demonstrate His power in your weakness. Then, finally:

Step Five: *Rest and release.* If you have been obedient to what God has called you to do in spite of your weakness, and you now believe that He will do what you can't, despite both your strengths and weaknesses, you can rest and release the results to Him.

You have put yourself under His power and protection, and this is the most wonderful place to be. You need to be attentive, because God displays His power in many different ways—some obvious, some not. Be looking for it. Stop stressing, stop worrying. You've done what you can do; now leave the results to Him.

At first this seems scary because you aren't yet sure how God will respond. But soon you will see His faithfulness on a regular basis. God loves it when His children ask Him to deliver them, to demonstrate His power in their lives so that they might tell others what He can do!

Do you know what I learned at the age of fifty-five? I learned that I was tired—tired of trying so hard and failing, tired of trying to be successful, tired of trying to be the perfect pastor, husband, and father. I was tired of trying to produce the "right" outcome in life, tired of predictable results, tired of my own feeble efforts at being what God wanted me to be. In short, I was tired of the burden of trying to produce for God.

And do you know what was such an amazing and refreshing revelation for me? God was tired of it too!

He had been trying to get me to stop for such a long time. So persistently, so graciously He had tried to get me to accept His power in my life. But here was the problem: I had always wanted to prove that I was significant in life *through what I accomplished*—and it just never occurred to me that my whole approach to life would displease God.

My premise—that I would be significant because of what I could accomplish—was thoroughly unbiblical. The Scriptures teach that I am significant because of what God has done for me.

My premise—that I would prove my significance by what I accomplished in life—was destined, if it succeeded, to glorify me. God created me to glorify Him.

"Well content with weaknesses . . . for God's power is perfected in my weakness." God provides us opportunity after opportunity to experience His power. We just don't recognize them because they come disguised as trials, problems, sickness, disease, loss, pain, hopelessness, and more. We simply see them as things we need to overcome, to conquer, to push through. And this brings us to the last thing:

Where should I seek God's power in my life? Here is just a short list to consider:

In offering forgiveness (Ephesians 1:18–23; 4:31–32).
In overcoming criticalness, greed, and anger
    (Luke 6:35–37).

In overcoming lust (2 Peter 1:4–6).

In lack of talent or giftedness for a task set before you
(Moses, Paul).

For courage in place of fear (Hebrews 11:33–34).

For provision and protection (2 Samuel 2:9;
Psalm 33:16–19).

In overcoming a terrible past (Joseph).

In handicaps and disabilities (Romans 4:19–21).

In despair and depression (2 Corinthians 1:8–10).

In trying to serve God and others (1 Peter 4:11).

In moments of personal weakness (2 Chronicles 14:11).

In protection from enemies (Psalm 44:6–8; 56:3–4).

In our prayers (Romans 8:26).

In empowering our witness (Acts 1:8, 1 Corinthians
1:18–19).

When exhausted (Isaiah 40:28–31; Ephesians 3:14–21).

With a difficult or seemingly impossible project
(Jeremiah 32:17; Ephesians 3:20).

In preaching or teaching (1 Corinthians 2:4–5).

For surviving and even conquering in trials
(1 Corinthians 4:7–10).

For being fruitful and effective and holy before God
(2 Thessalonians 1:11–12).

In short, you can seek God's power in your life *in any area where you need it*. And, friend, you do need it.

When I was a young man, I drove a 1969 Volkswagen Bug. It had a faulty gas gauge, and as a result, I was constantly running out of gas unexpectedly so that I would have to push my car off the road. A 1969 Volkswagen Bug is one of the lightest cars ever manufactured, but have you ever tried to push one—

up even a slight incline for, say, fifty yards? They are still really heavy!

They weren't meant to be pushed; they were meant to operate under the power of the engine. That's the original idea behind the combustion engine. You *can* push them. I've done it. And at the end of fifty yards up a slight incline I would be huffing and puffing and sweating profusely. But when I had gasoline in the car, covering that same fifty yards, even up a steep hill, was a breeze—because the power of the engine was doing all the hard work, work it was designed to do.

One of the reasons so many Christians are so weary is that they have been trying to push their spiritual lives up a steep hill—all by themselves. It's not that they aren't giving a good effort; they are giving total effort. But they are trying to do things by themselves that we were never designed to do by ourselves.

God. Never. Intended. That.

We need to exchange power paradigms. Just begin to seek His power in the issues you are facing right now. Admit that you can't fix it, can't make it better, and are tired of trying. Tell God you long to witness His power, not your own. Ask Him to demonstrate His power in your weakness. Ask Him to demonstrate His power in your strength. And see what you've been missing.

CHAPTER NINE

Expectations!

God comes in where my helplessness begins.
—OSWALD CHAMBERS

Dr. J. P. Moreland, in his book *Kingdom Triangle*, tells about the experience of a woman named Helen Roseveare, a physician from England who was serving as a medical missionary in Zaire, Africa. One particular night she had worked hard to help a woman in labor, but in spite of all she did, the woman died, leaving a premature baby and a crying two-year-old daughter. Helen knew it would be tough keeping the new baby alive, as they had no incubator, no electricity to run an incubator, and no special feeding facilities. Trying to make do, they tried a hot water bottle, but when they filled it, it burst. They had no other hot water bottles, so they put the baby as close to the fire as they could and slept between the baby and the door to protect it from the cold night drafts.

The following noon, Helen went to have prayer with the orphanage children who liked to pray with her. She asked them to pray for the newborn baby, explaining how difficult it was to keep the baby warm since the hot water bottle had broken. She also described the little two-year-old girl crying because her mother had died.

During the prayer time, a ten-year-old girl named Ruth prayed with the bluntness typical of children. "Please, God," she prayed, "send us a water bottle. It'll be no good tomorrow, God. The baby will be dead. So please send it this afternoon."

Helen gasped inwardly at the audacity of the prayer, but Ruth wasn't done. "And while you are about it, would you please send a dolly for the little girl so she'll know you really love her?"

Helen admitted, "I just did not believe that God could do this. The only way He could answer this prayer would be by sending a parcel from the homeland. I had been in Africa for almost four years at that time, and I had never, ever received a parcel from home. Anyway, if anyone did send a parcel, who would put in a hot water bottle? I lived on the equator!"

Halfway through the afternoon, while Helen was teaching at the nurses' training school, she received a message that a package had been delivered to her door. When she arrived home, she found a large parcel on her veranda!

"I felt tears pricking my eyes," Helen said. "I sent for the orphanage children, and together we pulled off the string . . . some thirty or forty eyes were focused on the large cardboard box. I lifted out brightly colored knitted jerseys, knitted bandages for the leprosy patients, and a box of mixed raisins and sultanas. Then I put my hand in again and . . . could it really be? Yes! 'A brand-new rubber hot water bottle!' I cried. I had not asked God to send it; I had not truly believed that He would."

Ten-year-old Ruth rushed forward crying out, "If God has sent the bottle, He must have sent the dolly, too!" Rummaging down to the bottom of the box she pulled out a small beautifully dressed dolly. "Can I go over with you, Mummy, and give this dolly to that little girl, so she'll know that Jesus really loves her?" asked Ruth.

That package had been packed and mailed five months earlier by Helen's former Sunday school class. It was God's answer to the believing prayer of a ten-year-old to bring it "that afternoon." In Isaiah 65:24 we read, "And it shall come to pass, that before they call, I will answer; and while they are yet speaking, I will hear."[1]

Helen's experience of God's power to answer prayer and provide was dramatic and clearly visible. Yet you too have experienced God's power in many, many ways in your own life, whether you realize it or not. But as God usually provides without sending us a text or leaving us a voice mail, we often don't recognize His provision when it comes. So for just a moment, let's think about the question:

How Can I Know If I've Experienced His Power?

The truth is that God has displayed His power in your life in many ways already. First of all, if you are a believer in Christ, God displayed His power in your salvation. In 1 Corinthians 1:18–19, Paul writes, "For the word of the cross is foolishness to those who are perishing, but to us who are being saved it is the power of God. For it is written, 'I will destroy the wisdom of the wise, and the cleverness of the clever I will set aside.'"

We aren't saved because we have finally figured this whole God thing out; we are saved because God interrupts our blind wanderings, even our antagonism, and draws us irrevocably to Him. The theological term is *efficacious grace*—grace that effectively and irresistibly draws us to God and salvation. "For I am not ashamed of the gospel," wrote Paul, "*for it is the power of God for salvation* to everyone who believes, to the Jew first and also to the Greek" (Romans 1:16).

God had to literally give you life and cause you to be born

again. Then He had to begin to change your heart to value what He values—again, through His power. If you are honest, you can also remember amazing answers to some of your prayers.

I remember flying in my dad's private plane over the Gulf of Mexico in a terrible storm; we were lost because our instruments weren't working, and we were low on gas. I prayed fervently, because my dad said we might have to ditch our plane in the Gulf. At the last minute, we reached land and landed at the airport. But . . . a few minutes after we landed, the gale-force hurricane winds caused the airport to flood and they closed it. If we had arrived only ten minutes later, we would not have been able to land!

I have a long list of answered prayers like that. So do you, I imagine. It is God's power.

God works in such a powerful way on our behalf—an answered prayer, a needed provision, direction, healing, hope when we are hopeless—and we rejoice at what we get, then quickly forget who gave it to us. *Observant Christians become grateful Christians, and grateful Christians become even more observant Christians, for they have learned how intimately God is involved in their lives.*

When we finally learn how intimately God is involved in our life, gratefulness is the only appropriate response. So, the question arises:

What Can I Expect?

Experiencing firsthand the power of God! That was a great true story we read about Helen and Ruth and the hot water bottle, but it wasn't your story was it? My favorite stories about God's power are my own—the times when I have experienced His power in such a wonderful way. We need to have our own stories. As Paul wrote to the Ephesians, "I pray that the eyes of your heart may be enlightened, so that you will know what is the hope of His calling, what are the riches of the glory of His inheritance in the saints, and *what is the surpassing greatness of His power toward us who believe*" (1:18-19).

I began this book with Paul's words in 2 Corinthians 12:9: "And He has said to me, 'My grace is sufficient for you, for power is perfected in weakness.' Most gladly, therefore, I will rather boast about my weaknesses, *so that the power of Christ may dwell in me.*" That's what God wants you to experience. His power *dwelling* in you, constantly!

Assurance of His power and presence! Paul prayed for the Ephesians: "That [God] would grant you, according to the riches of His glory, *to be strengthened with power through His Spirit in the inner man*" (Ephesians 3:16).

It's one thing to know God is powerful; it's another thing entirely to be assured of His power on your behalf on a regular basis in your own life. And to experience His *power* regularly is to experience His *presence* regularly. God doesn't dispense His power like an ointment on a burn, but from His presence within you.

Greater rest than you've ever known! So much of our stress surrounds our attempts to "fix things," to "make life work right" through all our efforts. When we can release the results to Him, and request His power, and then begin to see it, we can suddenly rest. God is at work.

It is believed by some commentators that Psalm 23, one of the greatest comfort passages in the Old Testament, was written when David was hiding from his son Absalom who was trying to kill him. Yet even in such a time of great danger, David proclaimed, "He leads me beside quiet waters, *He restores my soul* . . . . Even though I walk through the valley of the shadow of death, *I fear no evil*, for You are with me; Your rod and Your staff, *they comfort me*" (Psalm 23:2–4).

David experienced comfort and rest in the face of danger because he knew he had a good heavenly Father, and he trusted His power. You stop being afraid of the bully when your dad shows up!

Greater trust than you've ever known! When you begin to see God's power demonstrated constantly in your life, as Paul did, your trust in His presence and power in your life increases exponentially. Seeing God work in your life increases trust! You know He's there and He's involved. That's why Paul could say that, even though His thorn in the flesh didn't go away, he was pleased, because "*when I am weak, then I am strong*" (2 Corinthians 12:10). His trust had been transferred from what he could do to what his Father could do!

Complete surrender to His will in all things! How could Jesus, facing a crucifixion He didn't deserve, after asking that He might be excused from this terrible ordeal, confess to His heavenly Father, "Father, if You are willing, remove this cup from Me; yet not My will, but Yours be done" (Luke 22:42)?

When we finally understand that our heavenly Father is truly good, then we are no longer afraid of what might come into our lives, because we know that He is good and will provide for whatever we need. We stop being afraid of what He might do and start trusting both Him and His power.

When my children were small and had frightening nightmares, they would come into our bedroom. As soon as I put them in bed between Annette and me, they were peacefully asleep in minutes. They knew whatever evil was "out there" could not get past Mom or Dad.

Trust builds the ability to surrender to the One you trust completely so that you then rest completely.

Amazement at His glory! When you've witnessed the power of God regularly, your whole opinion of Him changes. It's one thing to read about what God can do; it's another thing entirely to see Him do it in your own life. To realize that the God of the universe is so intimately involved in *your* life! It causes you to be amazed at His glory—and His divine humility—that He would lower himself to be so caring and loving of such insignificant creatures as us.

Personal miracles! I've already told you how God healed my disease. But there are so many more examples of His power working in miraculous ways in my life. The power of God as He has taught me to rest and trust when for so many years I stressed and worried. The power of God displayed in my ministry, so clearly going way beyond what my giftedness or abilities could produce. His power in changing the lives of those I love as I sought Him in prayer.

I now expect, and see regularly, His power in my weakness. I expect and witness His miraculous power on a regular basis.

Seeing prayers answered like never before! It is imperative that we understand that God *desires* to demonstrate His power in our weakness. Once we get hold of that truth, we begin to ask Him more and more to demonstrate His power in our weakness—and He does. We begin to ask Him things we wouldn't before because our confidence in His willingness to help us was so low.

A faith that doesn't rest on what you can do but what He can do through you! Speaking to the Corinthians, Paul said, "My message and my preaching were not in persuasive words of wisdom, but in demonstration of the Spirit and of power so that your faith would not rest on the wisdom of men, *but on the power of God*" (1 Corinthians 2:4–5). This is where God wants to bring you. This is what you can expect as you seek His power in your weakness. "But we have this treasure in earthen vessels, *so that the surpassing greatness of the power will be of God and not from ourselves*" (2 Corinthians 4:7).

Well, then, if that's what I can expect, then:

What Must I Be On Guard Against?

Predicting the miracle! When we begin to call out to God for help, we often begin to imagine or decide what that help will look like—and that is what we begin to look for. That is a mistake. His ways are higher than our ways, and His thoughts are higher than our thoughts.

Sometimes the help you pray for and imagine will indeed come to you in the way you think it will. But many times the answer to your prayer for God's power intervention in your life will be so different than you imagine.

When Shadrach, Meshach, and Abed-nego cried out to God to help them when they were going to be thrown into the fiery furnace (Daniel 3), do you think they expected that they'd actually be thrown in but not burned up? Or that God would join them there? Did Jehoshaphat, when he called out for help, have any idea that God would cause dissension to destroy the invading armies coming against Israel (2 Chronicles 20)?

Don't try to predict how God will work. When you seek His power on your behalf, that power can come in such a variety of different ways.

Pretending you know what success really looks like! Paul asked three times for God to remove his thorn in the flesh. To him that would have been success—just remove the problem. It never occurred to Paul that adding something would be better than removing something.

Frequently success in our eyes is something that makes us look good; but success in God's eyes makes Him look good. Paul didn't need more personal strength or freedom from his physical disabilities. He needed to see God's power flowing like a raging river in his life. He didn't understand that at first, but when he did, he was so grateful he hadn't gotten what he wanted. What was best and most fulfilling for him was to see God's power launched in his weakness.

God has purposes for our lives and experiences we can't understand, so we'll struggle if we insist on God displaying His power in the way we are sure He should.

For Corrie ten Boom, success was surviving a German concentration camp with her faith still intact—not escaping the camp altogether—then using her experience to challenge and encourage Christians everywhere. For Joni Eareckson Tada, success was finding God's purpose and power through her life, not by being healed of paralysis, but through her paralysis touching millions of people as God demonstrates His power through her weakness. For Chuck Colson, success was not evading prison, but going there for his part in the Watergate cover-up. There God used him to prepare a ministry, Prison Fellowship, which has touched the lives of millions of prisoners and their families for Jesus Christ.

When you ask for God to demonstrate His power in your weakness, be prepared to accept that success may look different than you envisioned.

Wanting to take credit for what happens! When we experience a demonstration of God's power in our lives, we must be ever vigilant to give Him the credit for His work.

Here is the problem: when our faith is new, or just weak, we often pray with little faith or conviction that God will really answer. We are just covering our bases by throwing a prayer heavenward.

Maybe that's where you are now. You'd like to believe, but frankly your faith is weak. You're just not sure about all of this.

But even when you pray your small-faith prayers and God answers, your immediate response isn't always, "Wow, God answered my prayers!" More likely the response is a more tepid, "Great, I got what I wanted. How fortunate." Or you think, "This probably would have happened whether I prayed or not," or "The odds were 50/50 I'd get what I wanted anyway."

Because your faith is weak to begin with, even when a prayer is so obviously answered you may attribute it to luck. You prayed for a job and got one. You prayed for help and got it. You prayed for protection and received it. You prayed for health and got it. You prayed for an opportunity and you got it.

I seek God's power daily—and I see demonstrations of His power daily. Some demonstrations, as in the case of my long-term illness, took years, but most take a very short time. *Your mouth and your heart were designed by God to praise Him and give Him glory.* When you do it, you touch His heart.

Impatience! I had to learn patience through suffering in my illness; after all, it took twenty-eight years. But that patience also glorified God. Not in the suffering itself—millions suffer far more than I did—but to be able to glorify God in the midst of suffering. To be able to say, "Lord, if my suffering through this brings glory to you somehow, then I pray you will glorify yourself through my difficulty and give me the power to bear up under it."

Any sickness I endure is a direct result of sin in this world—sin I contribute to and participate in. That doesn't mean my gall bladder disease was a punishment for some particular sin, but it was the result of the very presence of sin in our world and its destructive force on all life, including illness and death. I have no special immunity from the curse of sin, and neither do you.

When the promised Messiah had not come after centuries of waiting, many stopped believing He ever would. But then, *"when the fullness of the time came*, God sent forth His Son, born of a woman, born under the Law"* (Galatians 4:4). In the same way, for your need and mine, there is a fullness of time. There will be a moment when God says, "Okay, it's time!" If we trust that we have a good and loving heavenly Father, we will know that the waiting, the delay, has a holy and essential purpose.

Living for anything more than the glory of God! When God created Dan Schaeffer, at a point in eternity past, He had one grand purpose in mind for me: that everything I do, everything I say, and everything I think will glorify Him forever. That is God's grand purpose for each of us. When we are seeking that purpose, surrendering our will and ego, as did John the Baptist so beautifully when he said, "He must increase, but I must decrease" (John 3:30), then God will be eager and active in demonstrating His power in our lives because He knows what we will do with that glory!

God does not make life complicated. We do. Our own desires, our own ambitions, our own agendas and lusts make us chase things that won't glorify God. This leads to regret and emptiness and ultimate failure in life because God isn't in any of these.

If you are living for *anything* other than the glory of God, you will end up empty and frustrated because you will be trying to satisfy your spiritual thirst with salt water. In practice you will be no better off than all those who don't know God and choose their own desires as they seek happiness and fulfillment.

Your greatest joy, your greatest fulfillment, your greatest purpose in life—the one that will bring you joy you have never imagined, the peace you've always wanted, and the purpose you've always sought—comes when you decide to live your life for the glory of God. When you do that, everything changes.

Everything!

In 1 Peter 4:11, we read, "Whoever speaks, is to do so as one who is speaking the utterances of God; whoever serves is to do so as one who is serving by the strength which God supplies; *so that in all things God may be glorified through Jesus Christ,* to whom belongs the glory and dominion forever and ever. Amen."

Embrace your weakness! From that place, God's power in your life launches! *Ask* God to demonstrate His power in your weakness and then *expect* Him to demonstrate His power in your weakness. Do it frequently. Make it a habit. Learn to rest in His power. And when you begin to see it and experience it—give Him the glory.

This is not just a new idea to think about, but a new way of living. Hopefully you now see it's the life God has always wanted you to live—the life of dependence.

Embracing our weakness. Finally, it makes sense.

DISCUSSION QUESTIONS

Chapter One:
Who Turned Off the Power?

1. "The fact that we have such an appetite for power indicates that it has not been a significant part of our daily experience."

   Do you recognize within yourself, especially in your most private moments, an inner desire for power? How does it display itself in your life or feelings?

2. Which would you say:

   a. I've experienced a lot of power in my life.
   b. I've experienced some power in my life.
   c. I've experienced little power in my life.
   d. I've experienced no power in my life.

3. In this chapter we talked about ways we feel weak. Which of those ways do you identify with the most? Why? Are there ways you feel weak that weren't mentioned?

4. How have you tried to overcome your weaknesses? What methods did you employ in your battle for victory? How much confidence did you have that your methods would

be successful in overcoming your weakness? Were you surprised at your lack of success? If so, why?

5. List the weaknesses in your life that concern you most. What are the top three?

6. It was stated in this chapter that "Personal weakness = Opportunity to experience God's power." As you think about this concept in light of your own weakness, does it make you feel

    a. Hopeful
    b. Doubtful
    c. Confused
    d. Suspicious
    e. _____ (add your own word)

7. "Therefore *I am well content with weaknesses*" (2 Corinthians 12:10). When the apostle Paul said he was "well content" with his weaknesses, he used the same words that the God the Father did when He said He was "well pleased" with Jesus. What is your initial response to the idea that you should be "well content" or "well pleased" with your weakness(es)?

ACTIVITY: Write down some of the ways you have traditionally dealt with your own weaknesses. Next to each item on your list, add how successful it was in helping you. Next, write down what you'd really like God to do through you in your personal weakness.

CHALLENGE: Using the above list, begin to ask God to reveal what He wants to show you through displaying His power in your life. Ask Him to show you more and more examples of how He desires to display His power in your life. Read and think about the Old and New Testament passages mentioned in this chapter.

Chapter Two:
We're Not Alone

1. "We can argue with ideas, we can challenge beliefs, we can roll our eyes in weariness at new programs and fads in church, but when someone's life is drastically and permanently changed, we have to pay attention." Try to think of several people you know who have been drastically changed by God. What part of the change God caused in their life impresses you the most—and why?

2. God hasn't called many of His people from the ranks of the strong and powerful. Read 1 Corinthians 1:26–29 again. What do the strong and powerful of our world see in Christianity that repels them?

3. "The power of Christ launches from our weakness, not our strength." Do you:

   a. Wholeheartedly agree
   b. Strongly agree
   c. Mildly agree
   d. Mildly disagree
   e. Strongly disagree

   Why?

4. Hebrews 11 tells of many who became mighty in faith—we call them heroes of the faith. Several were mentioned in this chapter. Try to think of three more people in either the Old or New Testaments through whom God displayed His power in their weakness.

5. Is there a time when you clearly experienced the power of God in your life? If so, what makes you believe it was God's power? Was His power displayed through an area of your weakness?

6. List five areas where you

FEEL WEAK AND INADEQUATE   FEEL STRONG AND CAPABLE

_____   _____

_____   _____

_____   _____

_____   _____

_____   _____

7. How hard is it for you to be honest about your weaknesses? Has anyone ever told you about a weakness that you weren't even aware of? How did you feel? How did you react?

8. In this chapter is a list of some of the areas where we feel we should be strong or where others expect us to be strong. As you look at that list again, where do you feel strong, where do you feel weak? Do you feel like a failure in any areas?

9. Can you think of other areas where either you or others have expected you to be strong?

ACTIVITY: Write down some areas of personal weakness where you would most like to see God's power displayed in your life. Limit it to two or three of the most important. Ask yourself how you *have* been dealing with your weaknesses up to now and how successful you have been.

CHALLENGE: Take some time to reflect and to ask God to begin to reveal to you areas of weakness in your life— perhaps areas you haven't thought of before or that you've tried to deny. Then ask Him what He would like to do through your weakness for His glory. As you work through this book, continue to ask Him to show you His purposes for these areas of your life.

Chapter Three:
Why It's So Hard to Admit Our Weaknesses

1. At the beginning of this chapter I quote author Lee Strobel as he relates an incident in his life where God used him in an area he perceived to be a huge weakness. God's power through his perceived weakness led him to do something he never would have done otherwise. Has God ever put you in a position where you felt very inadequate—and the result was a pleasant surprise? What was it, and what did you learn?

2. Author J. I. Packer wrote about "our fantasies of omnicompetence"—the belief that "I'm really good at everything." Can you recall a time when you thought you were good at

something only to discover later that you weren't? Was it a moment of self-realization or did someone or some experience make it clear to you? What was hardest for you to accept at that moment: that you weren't good at this or that you thought you were good and were mistaken?

3. Are you resisting the idea that you might be weak in a certain area? Have others talked to you about an area of weakness they see in you that you can't accept? Why do you find it difficult to admit your weakness? Is it harder to admit your weakness to yourself, or to others, or even to God? Why?

4. Read Romans 12:3: "For through the grace given to me I say to everyone among you not to think more highly of himself than he ought to think; but to think so as to have sound judgment, as God has allotted to each a measure of faith."

   Choose one of the responses below:

   a. I think too highly of myself at times.
   b. I think too lowly of myself at times.
   c. I'm not sure I know myself well enough to answer this question.
   d. I'm confident my self-assessments are accurate.

5. What is one weakness you can admit to that others might not be aware of in your life?

6. How have people or groups used your weakness against you in the past? Did that make you want to hide other weaknesses?

7. Has God been able to use you in a significant way in an area of your weakness? Explain.

8. It is often said that we enter areas where we feel a weakness in order to compensate for that weakness. Yet even with special training in that area, it still remains a weakness. Can you think of an example of this in your own life?

9. "We can operate in powerless mode for a very long time. Our results are acceptable to most—but if we were honest we'd admit to disillusionment . . . we expected far more." Is there an area in your life where you definitely thought you'd see more success than you have, especially given your training or giftedness? How do you respond to that?

10. "Our fear of admitting weakness is real, but so is the power of God available to us through that very same weakness." Do you find this statement:

    a. Very hopeful
    b. Somewhat hopeful
    c. A little intimidating
    d. A bit frightening
    e. _____ (Fill in your own response.)

    ACTIVITY: Take some time and prayerfully consider why it's so hard for you to admit weakness to yourself, others, or even to God (see question 3).

    CHALLENGE: Ask God to begin to remove the fear of admitting your weaknesses and begin to fill you instead with an excitement about how He might want to display His power in them.

Chapter Four:
Recognizing God's Power

1. "It is no small thing for the average disciples of Jesus to admit that they do not experience the power of God in their lives." Would you say that in your life you

   a. Experience the power of God frequently
   b. Experience the power of God infrequently
   c. Are not sure you've ever experienced the power of God
   d. Wouldn't even know what the power of God looks like

2. William Barclay wrote, "The Christian hope is not hope in the human spirit, in human goodness, in human endurance, in human achievement; the Christian hope is hope in the power of God."

   How much hope have you put in the power of God in your own life?

   a. Lots!
   b. Some
   c. A little
   d. Not much

   Explain your answer.

3. When you think of God's power in your life, in which areas have you expected (or hoped) to experience His power? Try to list four or five areas.

4. What do you think is the greatest example of God's power displayed in a human life? Why?

5. Have you ever experienced God's transforming power in your own life? Have you ever seen it in someone else's life? What happened and why were you so impressed?

6. "It takes an unimaginable power to change a person who is unwilling to change, resistant to change, or even hostile to change." Is there an area in your life that you can't imagine ever changing? Is there an area in which you'd truly like to be transformed? If appropriate, share with others.

7. Have you ever witnessed the power of God influencing events to accomplish His objective in your life, something that you thought was impossible? What was it, and what did God do?

8. We live in a dangerous world. Can you think of a time or event where you were protected from great harm in a seemingly miraculous way? Did you see this as a display of God's power toward you or as just fortunate circumstances?

9. How much are you relying on God's resurrection power in your life after you die? This is not an abstract question, but an intensely personal one. If we don't rely and trust in His power now, are we really trusting that He will/can raise us from the dead by His power?

10. "God's power *always* has a holy and perfect purpose. He cannot be bamboozled into meaningless displays of power. In short, God will not provide His power to accomplish anything that will not glorify himself."

Yet we often are tempted to want our own will to be done with God's power. Is there an area of your life where you suspect you are harboring such a desire?

ACTIVITY: God's power surrounds us on all sides, but we are often blinded to it, or we call it by another name (luck, chance, fortune, fate). It's time we start truly seeing the power of God!

Ask God to begin to make you more aware of the many ways He displays His power in your life and your world. And as He does that, begin to write them down or journal them.

CHALLENGE: God's power is just that—His power. It always has a holy and perfect purpose. It is not like a vending machine where we can choose what we want, hit the right button, and what we want suddenly appears. Yet God makes it clear that He wants to display His power in our lives regularly and powerfully. We need to be asking Him to display His power in our lives whenever He deems we need it most. Make that your prayer to God.

Chapter Five:
Discovering God's Power Points

1. Think about your personal history with God and write down a list of the things you have asked Him to help you with most frequently. Try to list at least five or six things.

2. Have you thought much about the truth that God made you to glorify Him—that this was *the reason He made you*?

a. Yes, I think about that frequently.

b. Yes, I think of it sometimes.

c. No, to be honest I don't think about this much.

d. Frankly, this is news to me.

3. How have you experienced God's power in overcoming sin in your life?

4. Are there areas in your life where you have been trusting in willpower or self-control to attain holiness rather than trusting in God's power to help you? If so, how successful have your attempts been? Is it your activity or actions that have changed, or has your heart been genuinely changed as well?

5. If you have ever told someone else about what you believe and what Christ has done for you, what did you really trust in while you were doing it? What do you think trusting in God to help you share your faith would involve? If you have experienced His power in sharing your faith, explain what happened.

6. When a person becomes a Christian, especially at an older age, it means that many things have to change. List the many ways that God would have to change someone's mind and heart to move them to true faith in Him.

7. Think about the illustration of the plastic pail over Old Faithful in this chapter. Discuss the power of sin in us and our feeble attempts to corral or control it. Does this give you a better appreciation of the power of your sin nature? What kind of spiritual pails do we often put over our sinful nature in an attempt to control it?

8. Read Romans 15:13: "Now may the God of hope fill you with all joy and peace in believing, so that you will abound in hope by the power of the Holy Spirit."

When you are feeling hopeless or in despair, do you ever consider that God's power is available to help you in or through those times? Normally, what is your first response to hopelessness, despair, or depression? How might you begin to ask God to display His power in those moments in your life?

9. "Jesus didn't pull himself up by His bootstraps; He called out in complete dependence upon His heavenly Father." In Jesus's moments of great distress and despair near the end of His life, how did He model for us the way we are to seek the Father's power in our own lives when all looks bleak? Try to come up with at least three ways.

ACTIVITY: Now that you realize the different ways God wants, and is available, to display His power in your life, begin to make a list of ways God might want to help you that you hadn't considered before. Keep adding to this list.

CHALLENGE: Ask yourself an important question: What kind of God wants to help me in all these different areas? How much more involved in my life does He want to be than I thought? What does this say about His love for me and His character? How is this beginning to change the way I view and feel about God?

Chapter Six:
Overcoming Our Own Resistance to God's Power

1. "It is not that our power is equal to or greater than God's; it is that we have chosen our own power over His." Can you think of places where you think you're strong, but where God may want to do far more through you than you imagine?

2. What are areas where (1) you feel a clear and obvious weakness, and (2) where you feel a real strength in your life? Try to list at least three of both.

3. As you think about your areas of strength, do the results of all your hard work seem to correspond to the effort you've put in? Would you say you are:

   a. Very satisfied with the results
   b. Satisfied with the results
   c. Less than satisfied with the results
   d. Unsatisfied with the results

   Explain your answer.

4. As you try to honestly assess the effort you've put into your areas of strength, how much would you say you were depending on God's power? What did that dependence look like? In what way did you acknowledge and confess that weakness to God?

5. Can you think of one particular area of your perceived strength where you feel let down or discouraged with the results, where your expectations were certainly not met? How have you tried to explain that to others and yourself?

6. This chapter talked about areas of perceived strength and, following Paul, we came up with:

    a. Apostleship—personal position
    b. Knowledge—personal strength
    c. Pedigree—personal advantage
    d. Righteousness—personal goodness
    e. Special revelation—personal experiences
    f. Miracles—amazing feats

    Which of these do you identify with most as areas of your perceived strength and why?

7. The chapter also talked about areas of Paul's perceived weakness which included:

Danger	Baggage
Stress	Fear
Despair	Abuse
Inadequacy	Poverty
Unimpressive	Sacrifice

    Which of these do you identify with most as areas where you feel greatest weakness. Why?

8. If you are beginning to sense that you have been unwittingly resisting God's power in your life, try to explain why you have been doing that. Make it in the form of a brief note to God—admitting your resistance and asking for His help.

    ACTIVITY: Write down some areas in which you are beginning to realize that you have been resisting God's power in your life. Add to this list areas where you honestly haven't been seeking His power because you didn't think you needed it. This may take a while. As new items come to mind, add them to the list.

CHALLENGE: Begin using this list as a prayer list. Start praying that God will change your heart and mind about your need for His power in your life in each of these areas. Before we can ever act differently, we need to begin to think differently.

Chapter Seven:
Understanding Past Disappointments

1. "Have some of your carefully created castles been washed away?" As you think about Jean Otto's confession, what are some "carefully created castles" that God has washed away in your life that have caused you great disappointment?

2. "When we do not receive what we ask for, we decide that God isn't really as good as we thought—at least not to us."

   a. I have definitely thought that.
   b. I have toyed with that thought.
   c. I have been tempted to think that.
   d. I have never thought that.
   e. _____

   Choose one of the options or fill in your own and explain your answer.

3. Can you list two or three things for which you have requested God's specific help and have not received the answer you requested? How did you respond to God about

each of these—that is, how did you feel about not receiving your request?

4. How have these experiences affected your fellowship with God? How have they affected your confidence in God's character and love for you?

5. As you revisit painful places in your relationship with God, in what ways does it *feel* as if God failed you?

6. In this chapter, "abundant life in Christ" was described as "finally understanding what life is really all about—glorifying God—and entering into that blessed state where glorifying Him becomes the great overriding purpose of our existence." Is that the way you've thought about the abundant life Jesus promised? If so, how? If not, what was your understanding?

7. Externalized Christianity is concerned about what's happening *to* me, good or bad, not what God is starting to do *in* me. What are your thoughts about the implications of that idea in your own life?

8. "When we try to deduce the character of God from our history with Him, we need to view it through the lens of His goal of transforming us into the image of Christ." In what ways, as you view what God *didn't* fix in your past to your satisfaction, do you think He might have been working on transforming you more into the image of Jesus? How?

9. List four or five things that God might be trying to prune from your life—*and why*.

ACTIVITY: This will not be easy. Revisit some of those areas where God didn't act as you hoped He would, where His goodness became suspect in your eyes. Be honest and be thorough. God knows these issues have been hard for you to understand. Bring them out in the open so that these wounds can begin to heal and so that you can renew or regain your trust in Him.

CHALLENGE: Ask God to help you regain the trust you once had in His goodness and love for you. Bring each issue up to Him in prayer. It's okay to confess that you still don't understand the why—but also thank God that He forever proved His amazing love for you on the cross. Ask God to begin to help you in this area of your weakness.

Chapter Eight:
The Rest-Release Program

1. If you had been in King Asa's place, do you think your response would have been different than his? How? Or how do you think it might have been similar?

2. Can you remember an experience in your life in which you, like Asa, felt weak and inadequate for the task you were called upon to perform? What was the great challenge, and in what ways did you feel inadequate?

3. Are you facing something today where you feel inadequate for the task (either vocational or relational) you have been called to perform? How have you dealt with such feelings of inadequacy in the past?

4. Are you a negative-reaction-first type of person when challenges arise or a positive-reaction-first type of person? Obviously we are not robots and might act differently in different circumstances, but what does the pattern of your life indicate? Can you see now how neither response is correct? Explain.

5. In what way does glorifying God seem to be the prime focus we need in order to begin to embrace our weakness? Why is it more important than anything else?

6. How does the idea that God created you for the primary goal of glorifying Him forever challenge your thinking?

7. Both King Asa and King Jehoshaphat were required to *do something*, even though God planned on displaying His power though their weakness. As you think of areas in your life where you want to see God display His power, what might God still require you to do in faith? Can you give examples?

8. Review the list "Where Should I Seek God's Power in My Life?" What would you personally add to that list?

9. As you ponder "resting" and "releasing" a particular area to God in order to see His power in your life, what do you think will be hardest for you?

ACTIVITY: It's time to fish or cut bait. Write down at least three different areas in your life where you are hoping to see God work greater through your human strength or where you are asking Him to display His power in your weakness. For each of these, go through the steps outlined in the chapter.

CHALLENGE: Even if your faith is weak, God will honor your requests. Remember, He *desires* to display His power in your life. Now ask God to help you see this happen. Ask Him to open your eyes to the various ways He might choose to work His power in your life. Most importantly, keep track of what you have asked God to do and where you have asked Him to display His power in your life. And when He answers, glorify Him! Praise Him! Tell others what He has done for you!

Chapter Nine:
Expectations!

1. We have spent a lot of time focusing on where we might have felt that God did not meet our expectations. Now let's take time to remember and praise Him for ways in which He has! Write down a list of the ways in which God has indeed answered your prayers in a big way, delivered you, provided for you, protected you, and guided you.

2. Using this list, begin to thank and praise God for what He has done for you. In each instance that He has helped you, praise Him for a particular aspect of His divine character (His love, mercy, power, knowledge, etc.) demonstrated on your behalf.

3. In this chapter we talk about the theological term "efficacious grace"—grace that effectively and irresistibly draws us to God and salvation. In what ways did God's powerful grace lead you to believe in Him, to change your mind

about Him, to change the direction of your entire life? What did He do and what methods did He employ?

4. "Observant Christians become grateful Christians, and grateful Christians become even more observant Christians, for they have learned how intimately God is involved in their lives."

   Are there areas in your life where God has done something good for you and you have failed to be truly grateful and thank Him? See if you can think of three or four instances. Take some time right now and thank Him for those things and confess your sin of ingratitude.

5. As you look at the list of things you can expect as you begin to embrace your weakness, which one is most important to you and why?

6. As you look at the list of things to be on guard against as you begin to embrace your weakness, which seems most important to you and why?

7. As you reflect upon all you've learned in this book about God, what has affected you most powerfully and why?

8. As you reflect upon all you've learned about yourself, what has affected you most powerfully and why?

9. What is the single most important truth you are taking away from this book—the thing that has changed your thinking the most?

ACTIVITY: Write down 2 Corinthians 12:9–10 and commit it to memory. When you are feeling weak and powerless, or when you want to see more of God's power and less of your own, quote it to yourself. Begin to apply these truths on a regular basis in your life.

CHALLENGE: Ask God to help you change the focus of your life—from living for your own glory to committing yourself to live for His! Ask Him to begin to demonstrate His power in your life over and over so that you may have more and more things for which to praise and glorify Him. When God displays His power in either your strength or your weakness, tell others what He's doing.

May He increase in your life, as you decrease. Enjoy your new life!

NOTES

Chapter One

1. Harvey Mackay, "Weakness Can Be a Great Motivator," *Orange County Register*, March, 27, 2000.

Chapter Two

1. W. H. Lewis, ed., *Letters of C. S. Lewis* (New York: Harcourt Brace Jovanovich, 1966), 250.
2. David Ray, *The Big Small Church Book*, "To Illustrate Plus," *Leadership*, Summer 1999, 77.
3. James Hewett, ed., *Illustrations Unlimited* (Wheaton, IL: Tyndale House Publishers, Inc.,1988), 242.

Chapter Three

1. http://www.biblegateway.com/LeeStrobel/2011/09/emerging -from-the-cocoon/.
2. J. I. Packer, "Rediscovering Holiness," *Christianity Today*, vol. 38, no. 13.
3. Joni Eareckson Tada, quoted in "My Heart Sings," *Christianity Today*, vol. 33, no. 1.
4. N. T. Wright, "For All God's Worth," *Christianity Today*, vol. 41, no. 12.
5. Doug Nichols, *Leadership*, vol. 15, no. 2.

Chapter Four

1. Philip Yancey, *Reaching for the Invisible God* (Grand Rapids, MI: Zondervan, 2000), 145–46.
2. William Barclay, *The Letter to the Romans*, quoted in "Reflections," *Christianity Today*, October, 25, 1999.
3. Henry C. Thiessen, *Lectures in Systematic Theology* (Grand Rapids, MI: William B. Eerdmans Publishing Co., 1976), 126.
4. Philip Yancey, *The Jesus I Never Knew* (Grand Rapids, MI: Zondervan, 1995), 182–83.

Chapter Five

1. Edythe Draper, *Draper's Book of Quotations for the Christian World* (Wheaton, IL: Tyndale House Publishers, Inc., 1992), #3469.
2. R. L. Russell, "Triumphing over Trials," *Preaching Today*, tape 119.
3. http://www.worldoncampus.com/article/religion/2011/10/ask_a_former_atheist.

Chapter Seven

1. Edythe Draper, *Draper's Book of Quotations for the Christian World* (Wheaton, IL: Tyndale House Publishers, Inc., 1992), #2798.
2. C. S. Lewis, *A Grief Observed* (New York: Bantam, 1976), 5.
3. Ibid., 43.
4. http://thechart.blogs.cnn.com/2011/10/25/steve-jobs-a-difficult-patient/.

Chapter Nine

1. J. P. Moreland, *Kingdom Triangle* (Grand Rapids, MI: Zondervan, 2007), 17–18.

Enjoy this book? Help us get the word out!

Share a link to the book or
mention it on social media

Write a review on your blog, on a retailer site,
or on our website (dhp.org)

Pick up another copy to share with someone

Recommend this book for your
church, book club, or small group

Follow Discovery House on
social media and join the discussion

Contact us to share your thoughts:

 @discoveryhouse    @DiscoveryHouse

Discovery House
P.O. Box 3566
Grand Rapids, MI 49501 USA

Phone: 1-800-653-8333
Email: books@dhp.org
Web: dhp.org